Written Communications
That Inform and Influence

The Results-Driven Manager Series

The Results-Driven Manager series collects timely articles from *Harvard Management Update, Harvard Management Communication Letter,* and the *Balanced Scorecard Report* to help senior to middle managers sharpen their skills, increase their effectiveness, and gain a competitive edge. Presented in a concise, accessible format to save managers valuable time, these books offer authoritative insights and techniques for improving job performance and achieving immediate results.

Other books in the series:

A Timesaving Guide

THE RESULTS-DRIVEN MANAGER

Written Communications That Inform and Influence

. . .

Harvard Business School Press

Boston, Massachusetts

Copyright 2006 Harvard Business School Publishing Corporation
All rights reserved
Printed in the United States of America
10 09 07 06 05   5 4 3 2 1

Library of Congress Cataloging-in-Publication Data

Written communications that inform and influence.
        p.   cm. —(Results-driven manager series)
      ISBN 10: 1-4221-0322-6
      ISBN 13: 978-1-4221-0322-7
   1. Business writing—Handbooks, manuals, etc.
      HF5718.3W78 2006
      651.7'4—dc22

                                        2006027883

Contents

Contents

Avoiding Grammatical Goofs and Gaffes

Introduction

• • •

As a manager, you're often called upon to produce written communications—everything from proposals for initiatives you're advocating and e-mails addressing key business issues to executive summaries updating your boss on important matters and technical descriptions of a product's features or a business process's steps.

Regardless of the type of written communication you must craft, you face numerous challenging decisions as you approach the task: How should you structure the information in the communication? What style and tone should you adopt? How detailed should the piece be? And how can you ensure that the final draft of what you're writing is free of grammar, spelling, and punctuation errors?

Answering these questions isn't easy. After all, there are seemingly countless strategies for organizing the contents of a proposal or e-mail. Moreover, written business communications demonstrate a wide range of tone and style—from informal and chatty to formal and authoritative. And rules for grammar and spelling seem to be all over the map. For instance, is it really that bad to split an infinitive or to end a sentence with a preposition, if more and more business writing is doing so? Given the immense variety in structure, style, and adherence to grammar rules in written communications, how are you supposed to figure out the *right* way to craft your piece?

Despite these challenges, knowing how to produce effective written communications is more important than ever for today's managers. Why? A skillfully crafted piece enables you to generate important business results for your organization. For example:

- You develop a persuasive proposal—winning funding for a new customer database that will cut costs for your company and enable the firm to deliver higher-quality service to customers.

- Another proposal you've written—this one for a set of services your company would like to provide to a potential new customer—stands out from the many competing proposals submitted by rival firms. The potential customer selects your proposal—and awards your company a lucrative contract.

- In clear, accurate language, you document the steps required to carry out a new vendor-evaluation process—enabling your employees to select the highest-quality suppliers for key business materials.

- You draft an e-mail to your boss updating her on the status of an important project. By avoiding common mistakes in e-mail writing—such as using dense blocks of text and neglecting to provide a descriptive subject line—you make it easier for your boss to absorb the information in your e-mail and identify issues that must be addressed in order for the project to succeed.

- You write an article for your company's Web site extolling the virtues of a new product that your company has just launched. The article proves so compelling that sales of the new offering accelerate.

But measurable business results aren't the only benefits generated by effective written communications: you also garner advantages for yourself when you know how to craft a written piece skillfully. In particular, you distinguish yourself from managers around you who *haven't* mastered the difficult art of business writing. And there seem to be more and more of them out there, now that many high schools and colleges no longer emphasize the importance of effective writing as they once did.

When you demonstrate savvy writing skills, you therefore build credibility and attract the attention of supervisors, colleagues, and employees. People throughout your organization view you as intelligent and informed. Result? More opportunities to advance in your career and to exercise influence in your organization.

But there's another benefit of knowing how to write well in the business world—and this one is more personal. The act of writing any business communication forces you to clarify your thinking about the subject at hand. Let's face it: you can't write about a topic clearly unless you know what you have to say about the topic first. Thus, producing a written communication gives you valuable opportunities to exercise—and strengthen—your mental capacities. And when you enhance your cognitive abilities, you think more clearly on the job, make smarter decisions, and produce higher-quality work.

Of course, the subject of how to write effective business communications is a big one, and this book can't possibly cover this ground completely. However, the articles that follow are structured to help you tackle the more common challenges in business writing. For instance, you'll find a section devoted specifically to proposal writing—a task that many managers find particularly daunting. Another section focuses on the question of how to organize the content of a business proposal. Strategies for selecting the right style and tone form the subject of one section. And another section explores ways to surmount particularly thorny business-writing challenges—such as crafting an effective e-mail, writing technical prose, creating executive summaries, and making your prose "lean and mean." The volume concludes with a section on grammar—including how to decide when to follow the rules and when to ignore them.

With these topics in mind, let's take a closer look at what you'll find in each section of this book.

Writing Persuasive Proposals

It's Monday morning, and you want to draft a proposal for a new project. How do you begin pulling your thoughts together? And how do you assess whether your proposal has all the right qualities and characteristics needed to persuade your audience to support your idea? The articles in this section provide helpful guidelines.

In "First, *Don't* Write an Outline," business writer John Clayton discusses the four distinct "characters" you must play during the writing process—each of which performs a different role: The "madman" brainstorms. The "architect" organizes relevant ideas into an outline. The "carpenter" adds structure in the form of sentences. And the "judge" rules on bad grammar or style. According to Clayton, too many managers jump too quickly to the architect, carpenter, and judge stages. He recommends giving more time to the madman stage—to generate sufficient ideas with which the other characters can work. During the madman stage, "you jot down things you want to say—lots of them, in no order, and with no judgments about their value. As you stoke the madman's fires, your creativity builds on itself. The madman works most effectively if he's just being creative—not also organizing ideas, completing sentences, or worrying about grammar."

The next selection—"Making Your Proposal Come Out on Top"—Nick Wreden presents the defining characteristics and elements of an effective proposal. For example, a strong proposal states the benefits of your idea in clear, compelling terms for your audience. It also follows proposal-submission requirements to the letter, saving your readers time and annoyance—and making them more likely to accept your idea. In addition, persuasive proposals present information from the reader's point of view and avoid boilerplate language—which most readers will dismiss as "junk mail." Savvy use of graphic elements such as diagrams, tables, and sidebars can further add to your proposal's persuasive powers.

In "Building a Bridge over the River Boredom," writing teacher Beverly Ballaro and business writer Christina Bielaszka-DuVernay define additional characteristics of an effective business proposal. They place particular emphasis on "the four C's of good writing": (1) *Clarity:* Your language conveys your ideas clearly and directly. Any jargon is instantly understandable by 99% of your audience. (2) *Coherence:* Your argument proceeds logically, and each section moves your reader toward your conclusion. (3) *Cogency:* Your writing persuades your readers to change their minds or their behavior—or both. (4) *Concision:* Your piece is economical. It does not waste readers' time or tax their patience with irrelevant or unnecessary information.

Clayton concludes this section with his article "When to Ignore Your Readers." In this selection, he recognizes the importance of considering your audience's needs while drafting your proposal—but cautions against going overboard with this technique. Why? Overfocusing on your audience can lead you to make damaging mistakes. For example, writers who try to "dumb down" their work in order to ensure that their readers understand them risk making their audience feel patronized and offended. And writers who focus too much on what their audience expects may end up using a formulaic approach that prevents them from thinking creatively. To illustrate, if you're editing a list of specifications that you copied from a previous document, the process may become so rote that you miss seeing fresh ways to improve the specifications. Result? A final product that's unnecessarily stale and perhaps even out of date.

Spotlight on Structure

Many managers find the question of how to organize their proposal's content particularly challenging. That's not surprising—since advice on this very subject abounds. The articles in this section present some of the more reliable strategies for structuring a business proposal.

In "A Winning Proposition," business writer Janice Obuchowski maintains that effective proposals must contain at least three major sections: (1) A summary of your audience's business need—such as a gap to be closed or a competency to be acquired. (2) A description of the results that your reader wants to achieve—and that your idea will enable him or her to achieve. (3) A solution that links your idea to your reader's specific needs—presented in confident language (such as "We urge you . . ." or "We recommend . . .").

In "Writing Well When Time Is Tight," business writer Nick Morgan presents additional tried-and-true strategies for structuring your proposal. He recommends first presenting your main point—in one sentence that articulates your idea and its benefits for your intended audience. For example, "A brand extension of our software into small-business finance will revive our flagging sales." Next Morgan suggests developing subordinate ideas supporting your main point. Possibilities for the brand-extension idea might include "All our users also use small-business software—we've got a captive market with 100% penetration" and "Our clients will associate the brand extension with our main software products and want to buy more from us." Finally, Morgan offers ideas for structuring your argument in the strongest possible way. Examples include presenting the problem facing your reader and the solution that your idea provides.

The final article in this section—"The Best Memo You'll Ever Write," by communications consultant Holly Weeks—lays out further tactics for structuring your proposal. According to Weeks, effective proposals briskly tell a story built around four elements: (1) *The situation—*

a quick, factual sketch of the current business landscape. (2) *The complication*—a problem in the landscape that unsettles the situation. (3) *The question*—phrased as "What should we do?" "How can we do it?" or "What's wrong with what we've tried in the past?" (4) *The answer*—your response to the question and your solution to the complication. For example: "Mediation's popularity has increased recently (situation). But because mediators possess varying levels of training, concern has grown over its effectiveness (complication). How might we address this concern (the question)? I suggest using our company's stature to spearhead a movement to professionalize the field of mediation (answer)."

Striking the Right Tone and Style

When you select a tone and style that support the purpose of your written communication, the document becomes even more effective. The selections in this section provide advice on ensuring the best possible match.

Business writer Richard Bierck starts things off with "Find the Right Tone for Your Business Writing." According to Bierck, tone is an elusive quality that determines whether you come across as a visionary or boor, whether readers are turned on or left cold, and whether they feel a sense of urgency in what they're reading. Two qualities determine tone: energy level and degree of formality. To select the right *energy level*, determine how "hot" your piece should be. Heat is conveyed through use of hyperbole, strong adjectives, and vivid images that incite your reader. A cooler passage is less alarming and thus conveys less urgency. To achieve the right *level of formality,* decide whether you'll use colloquialisms, which lend an informal air to your writing and can help you connect with certain audience types.

Consultant and executive coach Steve Robbins emphasizes the importance of using emotion to connect with certain audiences—especially those whom you want to support a major change initiative. Though Robbins's article focuses on face-to-face communication, the principles he describes can be adapted for written communications as well. Conveying emotion in a written piece creates a sense of urgency and enables readers to respond on a personal level. According to Robbins, stories—about how a change effort will affect your readers, about what the benefits of the change will be—can add a powerful charge to a written communication about the change initiative. For example, consider augmenting a videotape of an unhappy customer complaining about a faulty product with a memo or newsletter article presenting and analyzing an interview with the customer.

In "Rhyme and Reason: What Poetry Has to Say to Business Writers," freelance reporter Susan G. Parker presents basic guidelines for effective writing style—including simplicity, avoidance of clichés, use of active voice, and variety in sentence length and structure. According to Parker, trying your hand at writing poetry can help you master these elements of style—since poetry itself exhibits these stylistic qualities. If you don't feel like taking a poetry-writing course, consider reading more poetry to start incorporating these qualities into your business writing. "Poetry is more accessible than many people think," Parker contends.

Hallmarks of effective writing style include clarity and persuasiveness—qualities that the controversial and widely known novelist and nonfiction writer Ayn Rand consistently built into her work. In "Ayn Rand on Writing," business writer Theodore Kinni distills Rand's advice for cultivating a clear, compelling writing style. Rand's suggestions include the following: Don't complicate a simple thought. Don't use sarcasm, pejorative adjectives, or inappropriate humor. And don't use bromides. In addition, limit the theme of your written communication to a specific subject—and present a fresh point of view on that subject.

Of course, writing styles can differ markedly across different types of communications. How to be sure you're selecting the right style for a particular piece? John Clayton offers suggestions in the final article in this section: "When One Style Does Not Fit All." Clayton recommends matching the style of your written piece (as well as its structure and content) to the genre of your communication. Genres include internal memos, customer letters, proposals, and so forth, and can guide you in making decisions about style. For example, in many companies, internal memos follow a specific heading format and go to people who have some familiarity with the issues contained in the memo. Thus your style will combine strict adherence to heading format rules as well as use of acronyms and jargon that your readers will find familiar.

Surmounting Special Writing Challenges

In an age marked by increasing use of e-mail, economies fueled by high technology, and mounting pressure on managers to quickly absorb and act on the content of written communications, you face unique new challenges in crafting your written communications. The articles in this section help you tackle the most daunting of these challenges.

In "Don't Push That Send Button!" Nick Morgan provides suggestions for using e-mail effectively as a form of written communication. For example, since proofreading successfully on a computer screen is virtually impossible, avoid sending any e-mail that, for whatever reason, must be error-free. In addition, remember that even deleted e-mails can be resurrected and widely read by people you never intended to see them. For that reason, avoid sending e-mails that contain unsubstantiated information about real people or disparaging comments about your organization. Such missives could come back to haunt you someday if they fall into the hands of lawyers or potential employers.

If you have a strong background in technology or you

manage engineers and technicians, you'll appreciate the next article in this section: John Clayton's "How to Engineer Compelling Prose: Teaching a Techie to Write." As Clayton explains, technical people's focus on analysis and details can prevent them from seeing "the big picture." For example, "Say you want to make a compelling case for a bigger chunk of company resources. If the technical members of your staff can't persuasively articulate how their proposed projects will translate into bottom-line business payoffs, your bid is going to be dead in the water." Clayton outlines strategies for helping engineers improve their written communication—including defining audiences' needs for them, asking questions to encourage them to clarify their line of thought, and helping them structure, edit, and format their work.

Another especially daunting writing challenge takes the form of that inescapable executive summary you must craft—most often, for a proposal. In "Writing an Executive Summary That Means Business," Clayton affirms that a proposal's executive summary is "the one section that everyone will read." And he reveals the secrets behind successful summaries. These include establishing the reader's need, recommending the solution, and explaining the solution's value; using the right formatting and graphics to highlight your message; keeping the language clear, clean, and to the point; and adding clickable links that enable readers to jump to different information in the document if you deliver the proposal electronically.

An additional challenge that stymies many managers

in their attempts to craft effective written communications comes in the form of length restrictions: you're preparing a crucial report for your boss, and he has insisted on no more than eight single-spaced pages. But your draft runs twelve pages. How to pare it down to the required length? Clayton offers helpful tips in the final article in this section: "Five Quick Ways to Trim Your Writing." His recommendations include using tables to present compare-and-contrast information, providing graphics to capture complex ideas that would require lengthy prose, using shorter words and sentences, and selecting the one best example or anecdote to illustrate key points (rather than using multiple examples).

Avoiding Grammatical Goofs and Gaffes

Ah, grammar—that bugaboo that can put even accomplished business writers in a cold sweat. You want to follow the rules and therefore demonstrate your intelligence and attention to detail. Yet you know you're not familiar with all the rules. Moreover, you see others around you breaking well-known rules all the time (for instance, by splitting infinitives or using sentence fragments). What to do? The articles in this section can help.

In "Misused Words and Other Writing Gaffes: A Manager's Primer," business writer Kristen B. Donahue presents common writing mistakes and ways to avoid them. Gaffes include turning nouns into verbs ("This change will greatly *impact* our business," "We need to *architect* this new business model") and failing to achieve noun/pronoun/verb agreement ("The team [singular noun] send [plural form of verb] status updates to their [plural pronoun] project leader every week"). To avoid such mistakes, carefully proofread the final draft of every written communication. And if you're not sure of a rule, such as whether "team" is a plural or singular noun, work around the problem. For instance, write "The team *members* [clearly a plural noun] send [the obvious plural form of the verb 'to send'] status updates to their [clearly the correct plural pronoun for 'members'] project leader every week."

In "How to Write Correctly Without Knowing the Rules," John Clayton further examines the notion of working around uncertainty about grammar rules. If you find yourself using words whose meaning you're unsure of, recast to avoid risking a mistake. For instance, forgot the difference in meaning between "effect" and "affect"? Write "The *result* [not *effect* or *affect*] of the regulation will be higher costs." Uncertain of the difference between "complement" and "compliment"? Steer clear of both: Write, "I want to *praise* this team for its amazing accomplishment this quarter."

Despite the importance of following rules for grammar, spelling, punctuation, and style, sometimes ignoring the rules is the wiser choice—especially if doing so lends your written communication the informality and accessibility it needs to appeal to its intended audience. Business writer Christina Bielaszka-DuVernay addresses this issue in the final selection in the volume: "Is Following the Rules Tripping Up Your Message?" She presents four rules that, if followed slavishly, can make your writing stilted or ambiguous, and therefore ineffective. Take the rule "Never start a sentence with *and* or *but.*" Defying this rule can actually be a good thing. How? By starting a sentence with *and* or *but,* you may be able to break up an overly long sentence—and thus achieve more accessible, readable prose.

If you're like many other managers, you may always view business writing as one of the most difficult parts of your job. But that's no reason to despair. The articles in this volume provide you with a potent set of tactics and techniques for ensuring that your written communications get the job done—and deliver quantifiable results for you *and* your company. As you read the selections that follow, begin brainstorming ways to put your new knowledge into practice. Ask yourself:

- How effective are my written proposals? Do they generally win approval and support? If not, what changes can I make to ensure that they're more effective?

- How can I best determine which tone and style to use in a particular written communication? And once I've determined the most appropriate tone and style, how might I achieve it through my choice of words, the energy level in my writing, and the level of formality exhibited in my prose?

- What special writing challenges do I find particularly daunting: Preparing an e-mail? Translating technical information into everyday language? Drafting an executive summary? Meeting strict length requirements? What one or two strategies can I use to tackle my most difficult writing challenges?

- How familiar am I with grammar rules? Do I know which ones are important to follow, and which can be ignored for the purpose of more readable and clearer prose? How can I work around my worst "grammar demons" to avoid making embarrassing errors in my writing?

Writing Persuasive Proposals

. . .

You're sitting down to draft a proposal for an initiative you're advocating. How do you begin generating ideas? How will you know if the proposal will persuade your audience and be easy for readers to digest and thus to evaluate your idea's merits?

In this section, you'll find a wealth of recommendations—not only for generating ideas for content but also for checking whether your final draft shows all the hallmarks of an effective proposal—including clarity, concision, cogency, and coherence. One article even explains how to avoid going overboard with catering to your audience—which can lead to less-than-effective writing.

First, *Don't* Write an Outline

• • •

John Clayton

At some point in our formal education, most of us are taught how to organize our thoughts with a Roman-numeral outline—we're told it's the "right" way to write. But off the page, our thoughts are unruly, and they can easily tumble outside the boundaries of such structures. When this occurs, trying to start with an outline can contribute to writer's block—after all, it gets frustrating when the process doesn't go the way it "should."

That's why many experts suggest starting with something far less linear and constricted, with a far different format.

In a classic article on writing, Betty Sue Flowers identifies four distinct periods or stages in the writing process:

- The **Madman** brainstorms.

- The **Architect** organizes relevant ideas into an outline.

- The **Carpenter** adds structure in the form of sentences.

- The **Judge** rules on bad grammar or style.

What kind of writer are you? The answer is that you are all four kinds—just not all at once. Flowers argues that to write effectively, you must take on just one role at a time. For example, the carpenter can't nail boards together with the judge looking over his shoulder criticizing the placement of every board. The architect can't effectively use his design skills if he's also being asked to swing a hammer.

But the distinction between madman and architect is perhaps most frequently overlooked. Too often we expect our ideas to be born in logical order. We put a Roman numeral "I" at the top of the page, sketch out a first major point, and then hope everything else will fall into place. We're trying to organize our materials before we've generated enough material to organize.

Letting the Madman Roam

The outline phase gives shape to your ideas. At minimum, you need a beginning, middle, and end. An effective document needs a good outline, in no small part because that's what readers expect. But, notes Bryan A. Garner in *Legal Writing in Plain English*, "it's virtually impossible for the Architect to work well until the Madman has had free rein for a while."

> Your final argument should be linear, but your initial thoughts may not be.

In group settings, most people are comfortable with the concept of brainstorming, where everyone shouts out ideas, in no particular order and with no judgment attached. But far fewer of us are comfortable having our own individual brainstorming sessions. It feels self-indulgent, perhaps—a waste of time.

The madman phase is like your own personal brainstorming session, where you jot down things you want to say—lots of them, in no order, and with no judgments about their value. As you stoke the madman's fires, your creativity builds on itself. The madman works most effectively if he's just being creative—not also organizing ideas, completing sentences, or worrying about grammar. Most importantly, you need to not judge or restrict the madman's activities in any way.

The concept of "madman" may still sound a bit, well, crazy. But there are several concrete processes you can use at this stage to stimulate and develop ideas. Three of the most common are clustering, mind maps, and whirlybirds.

Exploring the Techniques

In *Writing the Natural Way*, Gabriele Rico urges writers to cluster ideas in a free-associative diagram. For example, let's say you want to write a proposal for your company to sell more of its products through online auctions. So take out a piece of paper and write "online auctions" in the middle. Think of this as a nucleus and put a circle around it. Now draw a line from the nucleus to another node holding the first idea that pops into your mind. It might be "expand customer base." Now you can draw lines out from that node with ideas on how and why the online auctions would expand your customer base.

A second major node off the nucleus might be "reduce cost of sales." Another might be a comparison to selling household items through eBay, a similar success story. As you brainstorm about eBay, you may think of additional considerations in expanding the customer base—so you can jump back and draw more lines off that first node.

Don't worry about what's a node or a subnode, or about whether a node such as "improve infrastructure" needs to be attached to "reduce cost of sales" or "strengthen tech-savvy image." That's going to be the architect's job, to move nodes around and draw additional lines between them. The architect may also discard nodes—but again, that happens later. When you focus on clustering, Rico notes, you "undercut tension, anxiety, and resistance. . . . If we are receptive, ideas come of their own accord. Clustering . . . generates inspiration and insight."

Unfortunately for business writers, Rico cloaks these ideas in talk of creativity and "the many-faceted crystal that you are." A more scientific approach comes from Tony Buzan in *The Mind Map Book*. Buzan notes that the neural structure of the human mind is basically a huge data-processing system with millions of nodes, links, and hooks. "Your brain's thinking pattern may thus

While you're "doodling" these diagrams, you're allowing your brain to take advantage of its full associative powers.

be seen as a gigantic Branching Association Machine (BAM!)—a super bio-computer with lines of thought radiating from a virtually infinite number of data nodes."

To express this "radiant thinking," Buzan encourages the use of "mind maps." He writes that a mind map has four characteristics:

- The subject of attention is crystallized in a central image.

- The main themes of the subject *radiate* from the central image as branches.

- Branches comprise a key image or key word printed on an associated line. Topics of lesser importance are also represented as branches attached to higher level branches.

- The branches form a connected nodal structure.

The resulting diagram is quite similar to Rico's cluster, with the subject of attention in the middle and related themes branching out from it. The difference is largely artistic: where Rico places each idea in an encircled node, Buzan likes to write on the branches themselves.

Additionally, Buzan encourages you to use images, colors, three-dimensional effects, and variations in the thickness of the lines and the size of the writing. He would have you revise and polish your mind map to the point where it might even be your final product. Flowers' stages apply here, too: the architect would be reorganizing the themes; the carpenter polishing the lines, words, and images; and the judge ruling on their beauty.

Though your audience would probably still prefer the old-fashioned written proposal as your final product, that doesn't make Buzan irrelevant. You can use the mind map at the madman stage—when you're literally mapping your mind. Then later the architect can reformat the mind map into an outline.

Doing What Comes Naturally

Both Rico and Buzan emphasize that this approach is nonlinear. That's the problem with starting with the traditional Roman-numeral outline: while your final argument should be linear, your initial thoughts may not be.

Remember: there's nothing wrong with this! The problem is not with your mind, but with the assumption that you should prematurely force it into the rigid outline structure. Drawing these radiating images or nodes is merely a way of keeping track of nonlinear ideas.

Garner notes that many lawyers use a nonlinear tracking system called the "whirlybird," which is structured much like a mind map or a cluster diagram. But rather than looking like neurons or nodes, Garner's slightly curved lines resemble the whirling blades of a helicopter or spinning toy.

Garner writes, "Once you've finished a whirlybird— whether it takes you 10 minutes or 10 hours—you'll probably find it easy to work the elements into a good linear outline. You'll know all the materials. It will just be a matter of having the Architect organize them sensibly."

As you consider clusters, mind maps, and whirlybirds, remember that you need not worry about choosing one technique over the other two. They're not really different techniques, but rather different representations of the process of generating and tying together ideas. You can choose any of them, or invent your own.

After all, it doesn't matter what your diagram looks like—nobody's going to see it! It's merely a tool to help you distinguish between your creative and organizational roles. While you're "doodling" these diagrams, you're allowing your brain to take advantage of its full associative powers. The result should be that your outline—and, thus, your final proposal—will be richer, fuller, and more powerful.

For Further Reading

The Mind Map Book: How to Use Radiant Thinking to Maximize Your Brain's Untapped Potential by Tony Buzan with Barry Buzan (1996, Plume/Penguin)

"Madman, Architect, Carpenter, Judge" by Betty Sue Flowers, *Language Arts* Vol. 58, No. 7 (October 1981)

Legal Writing in Plain English: A Text with Exercises by Bryan A. Garner (2001, University of Chicago Press)

Writing the Natural Way: Turn the Task of Writing into the Joy of Writing by Gabriele Rico (2000, Penguin Putnam)

Reprint C0208D

Making Your Proposal Come Out on Top

• • •

Nick Wreden

Nancy Sucher doesn't just read proposals. She looks for the start of a relationship—a partner who recognizes her needs and will speak to her clearly.

To Sucher, procurement negotiation manager at the $3.5 billion Boise Office Solutions, an office supplies and paper distributor, potential relationships start from following the RFP (Request for Proposal) instructions precisely. Not only do proposals that follow a different organization create more work for Sucher and her staff, they also raise a red flag. "If they don't listen to us—the customer—now, will they listen to us later?" she asks.

Selling may woo prospects, but customers are often won with proposals. Done right, proposals can be your best avenue to new business, funding, or opportunities. Done wrong, they are a waste of time and money. The key to increasing your winning percentage is bearing in mind the prospect's needs at all levels of the process. This rule applies as much to meeting the basic specs of the submission as it does to how skillfully you assess and respond to the prospect's needs. Ideally, this approach results in a concise, readable, and persuasive document.

Work from the Prospect's Point of View

Understand that while companies use proposals to underscore why they should be chosen, prospects, who face a pile of five, ten, or even more proposals, are actually seeking reasons to eliminate candidates. "Companies don't start by looking to select the best proposal. They seek to eliminate all those that don't meet their criteria. That means it's critical to make it as hard as possible to be eliminated during the initial review," says Dan Safford, CEO of the proposal-writing and training firm PS Associates. Let the prospect's requirements drive the process. Proposals should never be about what you can do, but what you can do for prospects. "A good proposal specifically addresses a prospect's needs," says Michael Kelley, a PricewaterhouseCoopers partner who specializes in global advertising, branding, and marketing. "A poor proposal discusses only your credentials." Never, for example, start a proposal by describing your corporate history.

Follow a Disciplined Process

A systematic, repeatable proposal process ensures that all requirements—and proposal budgets—are met. It reduces the last-minute rush that breeds ineffectiveness and errors. It contributes to accurate pricing so that the job is both winnable and profitable.

Following the right process can help avoid elimination. If you're responding to an RFP, follow its instructions to the letter. Sucher, for example, requires proposals to be unbound to speed copying and review. If the presentation requirements are not spelled out, call the prospect to determine the expected format.

Reinforce this with a prospect meeting whenever possible. Kelley says such meetings clarify the RFP, provide insights about the selection criteria and decision makers, and start establishing the relationships that can lead toward selection.

This process includes:

Thorough research.

"Spend at least as much time in studying, analyzing, planning, researching, and otherwise preparing to write as in writing itself," writes Herman Holtz in *The Consultant's Guide to Proposal Writing*. Research, backed by a clear understanding of prospect requirements, enables you to develop strategies, solutions, staffing requirements, and even pricing. Often it's helpful to show prospects initial efforts in these areas and ask for feedback, says Kelley. Such guidance can help ensure that your efforts fulfill expectations.

Timetables and an outline of responsibilities.

You'll need to determine timetables, responsibilities, and budgeting. Schedule responsibilities for key personnel, including managers, writers, and technical experts. Include time for multiple drafts, graphics development, reviews, and production activities such as copying and binding.

Careful attention to writing.

The most vital part of the process is, of course, writing. The proposal must clearly document an understanding of the problem, explain a solution, describe activities, and detail anticipated results. "Proposals are often won or lost on the effectiveness of the writing," says G. Jay Christensen, who specializes in teaching business communications at California State University in Northridge, Calif. "Use simple, conversational English, with one idea per sentence. Avoid jargon. Revise, and revise again, for clarity." Back up claims with case studies, research, or third-party recognition.

Organize the Framework

A key element of the proposal is the executive summary. Executive summaries are like movie trailers. They pique interest with appealing highlights, communicate the essence of the coming presentation, and help the audience determine whether to invest further time and information.

As a result, an executive summary demands your best thinking—and writing. Often, it is the only section read by decision makers. Within limited space, the executive summary must communicate key analyses, capabilities, and benefits persuasively enough to compel the reader to read the entire proposal. No wonder Safford calls an executive summary "an elevator speech in print."

"But despite their importance, most people do not devote enough time to executive summaries," says Christensen. "Executive summaries don't write themselves. They require an in-depth understanding of the proposal as well as an ability to succinctly communicate reader-specific benefits with punch and verve."

Executive summaries are neither prefaces nor introductions. They are not the place to introduce new material. Crucial elements of an executive summary include analysis, scope, recommendations, implementation highlights, and, most important, benefits. Length can range from one or two paragraphs to one or two pages. One rule of thumb says an executive summary should be 10% to 15% of the length of the proposal.

However, like proposals, the more concise executive

summaries are, the better. Use bullet points to telegraph prime concepts or activities. Avoid fluff like "We are pleased to present. . . ." Instead, point out that you propose setting up a European distribution network that can increase sales 40% by 2005. Says Kelley: "The more specific it is, the more they'll know you've listened and understand their problems." Don't be afraid to mention pricing; prospects will immediately scan the proposal for it anyway.

Experts debate about whether to write the executive summary before or after the proposal. Writing it beforehand establishes the framework and themes for the proposal. It also avoids the common trap of having the executive summary masquerade as a conclusion. Writing the executive summary afterward simplifies the capture of relevant points, primarily by culling key sentences. Consider combining the strengths of both approaches. Write an executive summary beforehand to crystallize themes and benefits, then revise that summary in the context of the final proposal.

Regardless of when you write the executive summary, start with a one-sentence summary that encapsulates the prospect's problem, your solution, and the benefits. Expand that sentence into about 100 words. Then add supporting points until the most important issues have been summarized.

Another valuable tool is the response matrix, a three- or four-column spreadsheet that outlines the specification, indicates compliance or another response, and shows where the requirement is addressed in the proposal. It can include a blank column for notes or checkoff. The response matrix is excellent for indicating where you have addressed important issues not specifically raised in the RFP. Providing summaries in the margins, as a college textbook does, also speeds comprehension and review.

The appendix, in turn, is an opportunity to expand or document points made in the main body. This material can range from brochures to photographs to even video. PricewaterhouseCoopers sometimes includes a CD-ROM with an organizational chart featuring members of the proposed team. Prospects can click on the name of a specific manager and see both a tailored résumé and a short personal introduction on video.

Other key tips for creating winning proposals include:

Personalize, personalize, personalize.

Proposals must be presented from the prospect's point of view. Emphasize specific benefits and value over your general capabilities and expertise. Edit standard résumés to reflect experience important to the prospect. PricewaterhouseCoopers even emphasizes aspects of its corporate history according to the needs of specific prospects.

Avoid boilerplate, despite its value as a timesaver. Boilerplate language in proposals is like junk mail in a mailbox—easy to spot and an easy excuse to discard the proposal. It also sends the message that you do not consider the project important enough for personalization. The only acceptable boilerplate is standard contracts, rate sheets, and proprietary and nondisclosure statements.

Remember that details sell.

Avoid generalities and hyperbole. Banish every "uniquely qualified," "extensive experience," and other vague braggadocio that undermines credibility. Instead of saying, "We will provide a useful manual," explain that a 50-page, 6" × 9" booklet will have an operational checklist as well as 10 questions at the end of every section to ensure understanding. Even avoid generic labels like "proposal." Instead, use a description like "a comprehensive program to improve quality through cost-effective inventory management."

Paint a picture.

Graphics communicate clearly and are particularly useful for explaining complex processes. Tables with features and benefits are especially powerful. Also use graphic elements such as call-out boxes to highlight key points. Summarize with bullets where appropriate.

Be concise.

Keep the proposal as short as possible. Some RFPs have page limits; make that an outer limit, not a target. It's tempting to add everything that a prospect might be remotely interested in, but such material dilutes your ideas and capabilities. One distinct benefit: short proposals usually get read first, which makes yours the standard by which others are judged.

Take Time to Assess

The proposal process doesn't end after submission. Proposals that have survived the prospect's best elimination efforts can generate an invitation to present. The prospect uses this opportunity not only to address issues raised in the proposal but also to determine chemistry and competence.

Win or lose, ask for a debriefing. Debriefings are vital for improving the proposal management process and bolstering your win-loss record. If you win, find out why. Which areas stood out, and which were ignored? "Client guidance after the contract is awarded can also help you execute the project more successfully," says Safford. Sometimes, clients may even be willing to turn over losing proposals for additional insights.

Loss debriefings are also valuable. Finding out why you were eliminated can strengthen future proposals. On occasion, it can provide a springboard to further work, especially if your recommendations or skills in a particular area were strong. "Both win and loss debriefings give me the opportunity to build a longer-term relationship, which is my prime objective," says Kelley.

Too often, proposals are marketing afterthoughts, left

to the last minute and filled with search-and-replace generalities. No wonder success rates suffer, and proposals get associated with uncertain return from extended effort. But well-written proposals can actually be your best sales tool—and the start of a long relationship.

For Further Reading

The Consultant's Guide to Proposal Writing: How to Satisfy Your Clients and Double Your Income by Herman Holtz (1998, John Wiley & Sons)

Reprint C0207A

Building a Bridge over the River Boredom

• • •

Beverly Ballaro and Christina Bielaszka-DuVernay

Beginning with a bang: good writers understand how important it is. But the best writers know that a catchy opening is only as effective as the text that follows it. After all, what is the value of hooking readers at the start of a report or memo if you let them go in the middle?

Crafting written communications that command readers' attention from start to finish is not easy, especially when the topic in question is complex or dry, or both. Here's a strategy that can help: approach the task by thinking like a speechwriter.

Skilled speechwriters understand not only how to grab an audience, they understand how to focus their message so that the audience stays tuned in till the end. They know how to use signposting and vivid language to make sure their message gets across. They understand how sayability contributes to comprehensibility.

Writing like a speechwriter can not only help you get your point across, but it also can help you get it across *faster*. And with time at a premium and managers always short of it, this is a major boon. Say you're preparing a report for distribution before a meeting. If it grabs readers at the opening and keeps their attention until the close, it can help you win hearts and minds before the meeting even takes place.

Here are some surefire speechwriting tips that can help you write to maximum effect.

Know Where You're Going

No piece of writing—whether meant to be read or to be heard—is effective if its author created it without a clear sense of its purpose. In such circumstances, the natural tendency is to throw a little bit of everything into the mix. But as noted speechwriter Peggy Noonan observes in her book *On Speaking Well,* "a speech about everything is a speech about nothing."

Imagine, she writes, that you are "an old prospector roaming the hills with a packhorse that carries your tools and provisions. If you pack the horse lightly you can move on and cover a lot of ground, maybe at the end hit gold. But if you put too many sacks on the horse's back it will collapse, you will literally get nowhere, and there's no bonanza at the end."

Is your goal to inform your unit about a change in company strategy? Inspire your direct reports to keep looking for ways to control costs? Persuade your boss to let you implement a new production process? Maybe your aim is to inform, inspire, *and* persuade. Whatever it is, write it out in a simple, direct sentence or two—doing so will ensure that your purpose is clear in your head before you start the hard work of deciding what is essential and what isn't.

As you work to winnow down your ideas to only what will advance your goal, take account of your audience, advises Alan M. Perlman, a communications consultant and author of *Writing Great Speeches*. How much background knowledge can you assume your readers have? You don't want to tell them things they already know, but at the same time you don't want to write over their heads.

Consider the Nobel laureate who once delivered a stirring autobiographical account of his contribution to famine relief that vividly illustrated the world hunger statistics he invoked. He had his audience riveted to their seats until he proclaimed, "How well I have learned my lesson from 60 years of incorporating and trying to maintain rust resistance in wheat varieties against shifting airborne rust fungus of the genus *Puccinia spp!*" The collective Huh?—though unspoken—was palpable.

Respecting your readers' level of expertise will go a long way toward keeping them interested in whatever message you are attempting to communicate.

Keep Readers Focused on the Journey

Effective speeches contain clear signposts that remind audience members where they've been, tell them where they are now, and point ahead to where they're going. Even as they keep the audience engaged and entertained, all the points tie back explicitly to the main point.

"One reason audiences glaze over and doze off," says Perlman, "is that their minds have to work too hard to make sense" of what they're reading or hearing. "The writing isn't sufficiently coherent; the linkages aren't specific enough."

One way to check that you've accomplished this is to boil your report down to an outline format consisting exclusively of the first sentences of every paragraph. This collection of lead sentences should read like a coherent, steadily progressing ministry unto itself, without significant detours or repetitions. For example:

Using in-house resources will reduce our marketing costs by 40% this fiscal year while improving our results . . .

To start with, the agency we are now using has raised its rates twice in the past three years . . .

Second, because of agency turnover, we have had four account representatives in as many years, and the client load of each rep has nearly doubled . . .

Finally, our in-house team has significantly grown in both size and expertise in recent years . . .

Another benefit of this change will be greater unit cooperation . . .

Make sure that larger signposts—those between sections, for instance—communicate to readers why the information following is relevant and useful. To keep readers' attention, speak to their self-interest.

Engage Them on the Way

Illustrative anecdotes, apt comparisons, and vivid imagery will make your points stick far more effectively than any dry recitation of facts.

"It's not a wise communication strategy to bombard your audience with a bunch of cold statistics," says John Treadway, president and CEO of Digibug Express, an online photofinishing company. "People respond best to life stories and personal experiences."

Speaking of a pitch he made to venture capitalists to

Get Out Your Squeegee

Before you actually submit any piece of writing, it is always wise to subject it to one final "squeegee" edit. Your goal is to polish the piece to perfection by making sure it meets the criteria contained in your final checklist, which you can divide into two parts.

The first half of your checklist should focus, at a microscopic level, on mechanics and style: Did you double-check the spelling of any words you were unsure of? Did you read aloud to note where your voice pauses naturally in order to figure out where to put commas? Are any of your sentences too long and complicated? Have you put quotation marks and apostrophes in the

support his company in its fledgling stage, Treadway says, "I could easily have restricted my presentation to abstract figures, such as the average number of minutes customers spend waiting in line at a kiosk for their photos, how long it takes to get photos in the mail—to detail the efficiency of the Digibug philosophy. But, instead, I chose to lead with a true anecdote I had picked up in passing from one of our potential investors. This investor's relative had recently spent the better part of two hours processing a large order at one of those self-serve photo kiosks.

"By focusing on a real-life example that all the busy, time-pressed people in the room could relate to on a personal level, I was able to illustrate in quick, practical, and memorable terms what my company is all about."

correct places? Do you have too many passive-voice constructions? Does every sentence make sense? Would someone unfamiliar with your subject understand what you are trying to say?

Once you have resolved these style questions, you want to step back and consider your piece from a telescopic perspective. The second part of your checklist should highlight issues of structure, clarity, and overall flow: Does your writing have a convincing point? Does it come to a coherent conclusion? do you offer your audience specific, memorable examples to back up the points you are trying to get across? Are your transitions between sections smooth and logical? Is your writing paced so that it moves the reader confidently from beginning to end?

And don't be afraid, even in a formal report, to surprise the audience occasionally. A fresh approach to a topic can really bring it—and your writing—to life. Think about how good speakers sometimes pique the audience's interest by throwing out a question whose answer proves surprising. For example, a speaker might ask audience members to guess the world's fifth-largest economy—after the U.S., Japan, Germany, and the U.K.—and then surprise them by revealing the answer to be not Canada, France, or China, but . . . California. This would get her point across far more effectively than blandly stating that California's gross state product exceeds $1.3 trillion annually.

Someone attempting to arouse the interest of potential investors in a line of innovative therapeutic devices

The Four C's of Good Writing

Thinking like a speechwriter forces a focus on the qualities that define effective writing:

- **Clarity:** Your language conveys your ideas clearly and directly. Jargon, if used at all, is instantly understandable by 99% of your audience.
- **Coherence:** Your argument proceeds logically, and each part of what you write moves the audience toward your conclusion.
- **Cogency:** Your writing is persuasive. It convinces readers to change their minds or their behavior, or both.
- **Concision:** Your writing is economical. It does not waste readers' time with irrelevant information, nor tax their patience with unnecessary verbiage.

could write, "In response to client and consumer requests, our company has come up with a line of products that will compete successfully in an expanding market." Or, instead, he could write, "What do beeping ladybugs, googly-eyed jellyfish, and robots dancing the Macarena have in common? They're all interactive toys for disabled children, created by our engineering wizards who've recognized a promising entrepreneurial niche." Which do you think would better grab readers' attention?

The more abstract the information you wish to communicate in your writing, the more urgent becomes the need to approach it from an intriguingly human angle.

Aim for Sayability

All writing—whether meant to be heard or to be read—
benefits mightily from the test of being read out loud.
"Where you falter, alter," writes Noonan, and it's advice
all writers should heed.

If you are like most people, you tend to subvocalize—
that is, you pronounce the words of whatever you are
reading silently in your mind. This buys you speed and
efficiency in processing information, but at a price: reading in this manner permits your brain to plug gaps, skim
over errors, and ignore awkward phrasings that will
become obvious to you when you actually say the words.

Ideally, you want to read out loud twice: first to yourself, for the purpose of identifying and cleaning up prob-
lematic sentences in the text, and then to someone willing to give you honest feedback. You don't need a detailed
critique from your listener; the most valuable—and possibly the only—question you need to ask is: "What stuck
in your head from the piece you just heard?" If your listener can't identify the main points you were trying to
communicate, you need to go back to the drawing board.

"Readability and comprehensibility are two sides of
the same coin," says communications consultant Perlman. "You're not going to get the audience to think or
do what you want them to if they can't understand it.
Clarity is the vehicle of persuasion."

Reprint C0501D

When to Ignore
Your Readers

• • •

John Clayton

Advice to business writers usually begins, "Think about your audience." The advice rightly points out that whoever reads your memo, marketing brochure, or grant proposal will have specific expectations you must meet. Most truly horrible writing fails to account for its audience. It's immature, self-indulgent, or (at best) simply irrelevant. All business writing works to achieve a goal— for example, selling a product or documenting a procedure. And achieving that goal depends on the reader's interaction with your words: the reader believes your product is superior or understands how to duplicate your procedure. If you've never thought about that reader—and the response you want her to have—your writing will not achieve the objective.

But there are times when you should ignore your audience. Sometimes thinking too much about your audience deadens your writing. The audience focus acts like a shackle that won't let you run. Unhooking those shackles—but keeping them nearby, because you'll need them later—can help you get where you're going.

This article examines five specific instances where you might be better off downplaying that classic advice.

Pinpointing the Wrong Target

If you're going to organize your message, content, and tone around a specific audience—as you should—you'd better make sure you have the right one. Technical jargon designed to impress the engineer will leave the layman baffled. But the simple layman's explanations will make the engineer yawn.

However, Laurie Rozakis, author of *The Literate Executive,* writes, "The person to whom you are writing is not necessarily the only audience—or the most important one." Rozakis points out that the *initial audience* (who asked you to create the document) may differ from the *primary audience* (who acts on your message), and both may differ from *secondary audiences* (who may offer suggestions or use your communication in other ways). Furthermore, she suggests that most documents have two additional types of audiences: *gatekeepers,* who can prevent your message from reaching its intended audience, and *watchdogs,* who examine your interaction with your primary audience.

For example, let's say you've discovered that an old friend works for a company you'd like to sell supplies to. Mindful of this audience, you fill your pitch letter with hilarious reminiscences about your off-color childhood high jinks. But he's only the initial audience: the primary audience is a purchasing agent who doesn't really care what the two of you did back in 1974. Your friend's humor-impaired boss may act as a gatekeeper and refuse to pass along such an immature letter. And your boss may act as a watchdog when she investigates the fiasco and reprimands you for writing a letter that had nevertheless connected with a specific audience.

You'd be better off ignoring the audience and structuring the pitch letter based on your product's strengths.

> Good writers do not "write down" to their audience. It doesn't work. Effective writers write *across* to their audience.

Writing to a Past Audience

Like generals planning to win the last war instead of the coming one, sometimes writers focus on a past audience rather than the current one. Your last grant proposal was turned down because it focused too little on implementation. But if your current grant proposal is headed for a different agency, that agency may care more about your track record, or your use of innovative approaches, than the nuts and bolts of implementation.

The big problem with past audiences is that often you're not conscious of writing to them. You end up adding all those details on project implementation to all future proposals because you don't realize that was a feature specific to a previous audience.

And the biggest problem comes when you subconsciously write to an audience from your distant past: the hypercritical English teacher. She put red marks over every paper you handed in, always identifying weaknesses rather than strengths. She insisted you use all the latest vocabulary words. She focused on mechanics, such as never ending sentences with prepositions, rather than your overall message.

Even now, every time you set words to paper you think you have to impress her. It results in a great deal of pain and wasted time as you labor to write. And it yields writing that's stilted, dense, and limp on the page.

But your old English teacher won't be reading your sales brochure. This audience may think a preposition is a perfectly good thing to end a sentence with. As long as the language is comprehensible, the audience is mainly interested in what your product does, not the mechanics of how you describe it.

Patronizing the Audience

Often your readers know less about the subject than you do. (That's why they have to read your material.) But when you focus too much on this principle, you try to "dumb down" everything, a process that not only frustrates you, but also rarely helps the reader.

In *The Craft of Revision,* Donald M. Murray says that good writers "do not 'write down' to their audience. It doesn't work. Effective writers write *across* to their audience."

Your readers can tell if you think they're stupid. And they'll resent it. So instead of considering them a "weakest link," think of your readers as not yet having learned certain acronyms or been exposed to certain concepts. They're just like you were before you acquired this body of knowledge. Thus, Murray recommends writing for yourself: effective writers, he says, "think and feel the way their readers feel; they do not stand apart [from] but beside their readers." And when good writers review what they've written, they trust themselves to talk back,

> When you write, don't get bogged down analyzing the audience's level of experience or intelligence. Save that for the revision process.

saying, "Hey, slow down!" or "You've lost me," or "That's great, do more of that."

Thus, as you document your bank's credit approval process, steer clear of oversimplified metaphors ("This loan is like your allowance"). Instead picture yourself applying for a loan and write what you would want to know.

When you write, don't get bogged down analyzing the audience's level of experience or intelligence. Save that for the revision process, when you should study each concept and word, making sure you've given the audience enough context, explanation, and space to understand it.

Forgoing Attitude for Craft

Writing—even the most pragmatic technical writing—is an inherently individual, even creative, process. When you put words together, you do so uniquely, based on your personality. And when the reader reads those words, she sees behind them (perhaps subconsciously) your personality and attitude. When she can't sense your presence within the words, she may stop reading.

Thus, if you focus so much on the audience that you suppress yourself, you will not connect with that audience.

William Zinsser, author of *On Writing Well,* says that writing involves both craft and attitude. "In terms of craft, there is no excuse for losing the reader through sloppy workmanship. If he drowses off . . . because you have been careless about a technical detail, the fault is entirely yours." But, he says, when it comes to your attitude, you must relax and say what you want to say. If you lose the reader because he doesn't like you or what you are saying, then so be it.

The grant proposal you are writing will fund a program that you believe in. When you relax and let that show, your writing comes alive and your audience believes in it as you do—*because* you do. If you focus only on your readers, you won't be able to show them why to believe.

Again, during revision these may be very appropriate issues to examine. "Is there too much of me in here?" "Am I really connecting with this particular agency?" But when you write the first draft, you're better off expressing yourself and your attitude than focusing solely on the audience.

Substituting Formula for Thought

For most people, writing and thinking are interlinked. As you write a particular specification for software your company will create, you realize how this issue affects another part of the software. You didn't realize it in the development meeting or while you were fooling around with the prototype. There's nothing wrong with this—indeed it's very beneficial. But it means your brain must be turned on while you're writing.

However, too much focus on what the audience expects may result in a formula or template you feel you must meet. You may even be editing a file you copied over from the previous set of specifications. And it may become so rote that you never turn on your brain—and so you never realize the implications, and the software suffers for it.

Alternatively, you may be so intimidated by the formula that you dare not change it enough to meet the needs of the moment. For example, if you're writing your first press release, and you have three previous ones sitting on your desk as models, you may get so caught up in mimicking the style (the dateline, the short paragraphs, the who-what-where-when) that you end up blandly parroting them. You never get to explain why it matters—indeed, you may not have been able to figure that out for yourself.

Whatever you're writing about, you must first clarify your train of thought on it. Then you can direct that train toward an audience.

Good writers usually have a clear idea of their audience. But they also have a certain self-confidence: a knowledge that the words come from inside them, their experiences, and their expertise.

For Further Reading

The Craft of Revision by Donald M. Murray (2000, Harcourt Brace Jovanovich)

The Literate Executive by Laurie Rozakis, Ph.D. (2000, McGraw-Hill)

On Writing Well: The Classic Guide to Writing Nonfiction by William Zinsser (2001, Harper Resource)

Reprint C0112B

Spotlight on Structure

· · ·

Many managers find the question of how to organize their proposal's content particularly challenging. That's not surprising—since advice on this very subject abounds. The articles in this section present some of the more reliable strategies for structuring a business proposal.

Though the writers of these selections offer a variety of ideas, common themes emerge in their recommendations. For example, they all agree that it's important to state your understanding of your reader's concern, problem, or challenge early in your proposal. Additional required components include your proposed solution—presented in clear, confident language—as well as subordinate points that support your main argument.

A Winning Proposition

• • •

Janice Obuchowski

"Although good proposals by themselves seldom win deals," writes proposal consultant Tom Sant, "bad proposals can definitely lose them."

The single biggest mistake that you can make when writing a proposal is to tell your prospect all about your company. In fact, effective proposals are not about *your* business, Sant points out, they're about your prospective *customer's* business. In *Persuasive Business Proposals: Writing to Win More Customers, Clients, and Contracts,* Sant offers step-by-step guidance in crafting customer-focused proposals that win business.

Write with a Purpose

Telling people they have to put together a business proposal, writes Sant, "is like turning on the lights in a dark room and watching the cockroaches scatter." Businesspeople will resort to all sorts of expedients to avoid writing customer-focused content. They'll clone old proposals, changing company names and updating basic information. Or they'll do a "data dump," gathering all the internal marketing information they can find.

But your prospects aren't interested in bulk or irrelevant detail, and they certainly don't want to have to work to understand what your company can offer them.

The Seven Deadly Sins of Proposal Writing

1. Failure to focus on the client's business problems and payoffs; the content sounds generic.
2. No persuasive structure—the proposal is an "information dump."
3. No clear differentiation of this customer compared with other customers.
4. Failure to offer a compelling value proposition.
5. Key points are buried—no punch, no highlighting.
6. Key points are difficult to read because they're full of jargon, too long, or too technical.
7. Credibility killers—misspellings, grammar and punctuation errors, use of the wrong client's name, inconsistent formatting, and similar mistakes.

What they want are solutions, clearly and compellingly presented.

The bottom line, Sant writes, is that a proposal is a sales document. To convince prospective clients to choose your products and services, you must articulate to them that you have a solution to their business problem and that you can provide value. In short, you must be persuasive.

The Four Steps of Persuasion

Persuasive writing is one of the toughest communication challenges to master. When you're under stress (the proposal deadline is looming), you're likely to revert to presenting information in the way that feels best to you rather than presenting it as the prospect would like to receive it.

Sant suggests taking a tip from journalism and using a funnel-writing technique: start with the fact or set of facts most important to the reader and then move on to the next most important fact, and so on. By structuring your document this way, you allow readers to stop reading as soon as they've assimilated enough information.

The challenge, then, becomes figuring out the most important facts from the prospect's perspective. Sant offers this four-step process to help:

1. Understand the customer's needs and problems.

"Summarize the business situation briefly, focusing on the gap to be closed or the competency to be acquired,"

Seven Questions for a Client-Centered Proposal

"Before you ever set pencil to paper," Sant writes, "before your fingertips caress a single key, you should answer the following seven questions. They'll force you to develop a client-centered perspective."

1. **What is the client's problem or need?** Whether the potential client has issued a specific request or you're proactively offering a solution, don't confuse what you can give the client with what the client can get out of it.

2. **What makes this problem worth solving?** What makes this need worth addressing? Evaluate carefully. Ask yourself, Why now? What makes this a situation that can't be ignored, and what makes it the right time to act?

3. **What goals must be served by whatever action is taken?** Before you propose anything, make sure you understand the standards by which the prospective customer judges success. What is it trying to accomplish? What is it trying to avoid?

4. **Which goal has the highest priority?** After you've established the customer's desired outcomes, determine which ones matter most. Then, in your proposal, present them in that order—from greatest to least importance—establishing that you understand how the company thinks.

5. **What products/applications/services can I offer that will solve the problem or meet the need?** Typically, a problem can be solved in several ways. Look at all the approaches. The more creative you

are in combining what you have to offer with what you know about the client's needs, the more likely you'll be able to distinguish your offer from the rest of the pack.

6. **What results are likely to follow from each potential recommendation?** Make an educated guess, basing it on your prior experiences. Will your recommendations lead to the client's most important goals? What will they cost?

7. **Comparing these results with the customer's desired outcomes or goals, which recommendation is best?** Choose the option that would be best for the client, and use that as the basis of your proposal. Resist the temptation to recommend a solution that simply gives you the highest profit margin (or advantage). Think long term. Hopefully you're establishing a relationship that will be sustained.

he writes. By demonstrating that you've listened to the client team and understand their needs, you help them feel confident that your offerings will be right for their company.

2. Focus on the results the customer wants to achieve.

How does the prospective client measure success? What kind of results does the prospective customer need to see for your products and services to seem desirable?

Although it might seem more intuitive to state the problem and then offer the solution, remember that the goal is to motivate and that the problem might not be motivation enough.

"Most businesses are faced with dozens and dozens of problems or needs, most of which will never get solved," Sant writes. Why? Because solving the problem doesn't seem worth the effort. You are striving to convince the customer that the problem you are addressing is one that needs to be fixed.

3. Recommend a solution.

Incredibly, most proposals neglect this step. Instead, they simply describe their products and services without ever linking them to the customer's specific needs. Don't be passive when you recommend a solution. Use language such as "we recommend" or "we urge you" to get your point across in a strong, positive way. The customer must be convinced that the payoff will be large.

And you need to prove you're capable of implementing your solution—that you can get it done on time and on budget. So include references, testimonials, or case studies. But remember that less is more here. One glowing testimonial is better than a smattering of less convincing material.

4. Keep it simple.

It's easy to forget that clients are not as familiar with your work as you are. Don't make the mistake of confusing readers or of losing their attention by distracting them with too much technical detail or jargon. Make your proposal as short, concise, and clear as possible. Use illustrations and avoid acronyms whenever you can.

And try to keep your sentences short. Aim for 15 to 18 words per sentence. When you are describing processes, do so in a simple step-by-step fashion, highlighting all your main points as you go. Boldface type, headings, bullet points, and white space will help you clarify your ideas. The more readable your proposal, the better your chances that the prospect will become a client.

Reprint C0507D

Writing Well
When Time
Is Tight

• • •

Nick Morgan

It's 2 A.M. the night before you have to present your
strategy for reviving slumping sales. You've come up
with nothing all these weeks—until now. Eureka! It's all
about brand extension, you suddenly realize, and tomor-
row you're going to stand before the board and suggest—
intelligent toothpaste.

Yes, intelligent toothpaste. Your little software company will market a brand of toothpaste containing a
chip that dispenses instructions for better brushing and

reorders the toothpaste when the tube is low. You'll need to set up joint partnership agreements with Wal-Mart and FedEx, but you'll write out the details of that later. Right now it's time to get your proposal written and time's in short supply. And writing was never your best subject.

Here's a three-step fast writing process that will help you express yourself clearly. If you find yourself with time later to add some polish, great. But when your chief goals are speed and clarity, it will get the job done.

First, formulate a thesis, or main point.

This should be one sentence that articulates the idea and its benefits for the intended audience. In this case, the thesis might be something like:

A brand extension of our software into intelligent toothpaste will revive our flagging sales.

Note that the thesis doesn't capture the full richness and scope of the idea. It doesn't mention the joint partnerships with Wal-Mart and FedEx, for example, nor does it explain what intelligent toothpaste might actually be. But it does detail the benefit that the audience—the board—expects to hear. Note too that the concept and its benefit are directly, not indirectly, linked. Such clarity and simplicity are essential to good thesis writing.

Next, develop subordinate ideas that support your thesis.

Here are a few possibilities:

All our users also use toothpaste—we've got a captive market with 100% penetration.

Remembering to buy toothpaste before the tube runs out is a tiresome chore.

Consumers will love a talking tube of toothpaste.

Our clients will associate fresh breath with our software and therefore want to buy more of our products.

Now you've got four subordinate ideas here. But what order should you put them in? What's the glue that will hold them together?

Finally, choose the best structure for your argument.

Now it's time to choose the organizational principle that will allow you to structure your argument in the strongest possible way. Here are four basic organizational principles you might use; which is best depends on the nature of your argument.

Problem/Solution

Often the strongest way to organize an argument quickly, problem/solution is easy to follow because it corresponds to a common thought process.

In this case, only one of the subordinate ideas is a problem: *Remembering to buy toothpaste before the tube runs out is a tiresome chore.* The others are neither problems nor solutions to the problem identified. So you have to identify other problems to which the subordinate ideas will serve as solutions:

Our sales are flagging.

—We can really boost our sales by extending our brand into the lucrative toothpaste market because all our users also use toothpaste.

Consumers interact with our current products only when they're working at their PCs; we need our brand to touch their personal as well as their professional lives.

—After our clients buy our intelligent toothpaste, they will associate our software with the pleasant, confident feeling having fresh breath gives them; they'll therefore want to buy more of our products.

Remembering to buy toothpaste before the tube runs out is a tiresome chore.

—Our intelligent toothpaste will ensure that our customers always have toothpaste on hand; they'll appreciate this convenience.

It's hard to get consumers' attention in the crowded high-tech marketplace.

—A talking tube of toothpaste will get their notice because it's new, different, and technologically sophisticated.

Cause/Effect

This organizational principle can also be quite effective, but among the subordinate ideas there are no causes, only effects. Thus these ideas will have to be reworked to strengthen the connections among them:

We have an information database of all our users.

Because they're aware of the importance of good dental hygiene, they all use toothpaste.

They each face the daily challenge of ensuring they have toothpaste on hand.

If we can meet that challenge by making it easy for them to accomplish this small but vital need, our users will be grateful and will begin to love our talking tube.

In addition, they will associate our brand with fresh breath.

They will therefore have positive associations that will lead them to want to buy more of our products.

Comparison/Contrast

Using comparison/contrast is a good way to highlight the advantages of one model while pointing out the disadvantages of another. In this case, you're going to show how marketing intelligent toothpaste provides more benefits than the idea currently on the table: launching an e-mail campaign using rented lists.

What features do these plans have in common? This is the "compare" part of your argument. In this case, it's pretty simple: Both aim to increase sales. But that's where the similarity ends. You might begin this way:

The brand extension plan and the e-mail marketing plan have a common goal: reviving flagging sales.

Now it's time to go into the "contrast" part of your argument. Here's where you hit your subordinate ideas one by one, building on their benefits while demonstrating the inferiority of the other plan:

All our users also use toothpaste—we've got a captive market with 100 percent penetration. In targeting this market, we're reaching out to people who know us and our products well. We can't expect anything close to this level of brand recognition among those on the rented e-mail lists. And given the level of spam these days, sending out this e-mail could actually damage our credibility with those who do know us.

Remembering to buy toothpaste before the tube runs out is a tiresome chore. Not only will our intelligent toothpaste ensure that our customers never run out of toothpaste, it will also save them the time they would have spent going to the store to buy more. But it's likely that many people who receive our e-mail will perceive it as a waste of time.

As much as we dress up a marketing e-mail with bells and whistles, we're not reaching people in a new way; the technology is old hat. But a talking tube of toothpaste—that's seriously cutting-edge. It has a fun, trendy feel and the potential to become a status item among a highly desirable demographic. The status we gain from this innovative product will enhance the reputation of our other offerings.

Our clients will associate fresh breath and cutting-edge technology with our products and will want to buy more. In contrast, a marketing e-mail offers nothing special for the customer to associate with our products; indeed, those who perceive the e-mail as a nuisance could come to perceive our *products* as nuisances.

Chronology

Arguments structured along chronological lines can highlight the time and data that have already gone into a project. Say, for instance, that your little software company had previously extended its brand into auxiliary consumer products such as talking stuffed animals. A chronological presentation of when the various steps of that process were made and what the results were could help you make your argument as to why extending the brand into intelligent toothpaste is a good idea and why doing it right now is sound business strategy. Arranging handout material chronologically might also make sense, even if you've ordered your argument using one of the other organizing principles.

Once you've put your subordinate ideas together in one of these four ways, you need to flesh out details that will strengthen your argument. Use the main thesis as a check—include nothing that does not support it. Your thesis should be the topic sentence of your first paragraph, and the subordinate ideas, perhaps with some modification, should be the topic sentences for succeeding paragraphs. Then all that's left to do is construct a quick close that reinforces the big ideas in your strategy and seeks the audience's commitment to it.

The document you have once you've completed this process may or may not be rhetorically elegant, but it will be clear and logically sound. And that's a good start.

Reprint C0205B

The Best Memo You'll Ever Write

• • •

Holly Weeks

There is a lot of advice out there about what defines good business writing, much of it conflicting. Business readers like writing that is clear, but writers are often encouraged to make their information "sound good." Readers want their information served up simply and directly, but writers are pushed to make their copy "stand out." Readers want to get to the bottom line fast, but writers are criticized if they leave out background detail that someone might look for.

Conflicting advice is hard to follow, and clarity can be the first standard to fall. Not because the writer's thinking is fuzzy—a frequent disparagement—or because the writer is intellectually dishonest and trying to hide the truth behind smudgy language, but because the writer is trying to juggle contradictory ideas about style, presentation, and level of detail.

The truth is that there is a better way to approach business writing, and that is to start from these three realities: business readers are content driven, time pressed, and in search of solutions.

What does that mean to writers? First, they should get out of the impressive-language business. To content-driven readers, language simply carries information, ideas, and the relationships among them. Good language is rather like a good butler—it works smoothly in the service of the reader without calling attention to itself. Second, organization is critical. Whatever particular analysis you make or actions you advocate, how compelling readers will find your report or memo depends largely on how logically you order and present information and ideas.

The Starting Point

From your introduction the content-driven reader judges whether the rest of your memo is worth his time. Yet the beginning is where many writers ease in and build slowly.

This is a mistake. Your opening must answer the reader's question "Why am I reading this?" To do so, it needs to establish the relevance and the utility of the document as a whole. Here is where the classic business writing text *The Minto Pyramid Principle: Logic in Writing, Thinking and Problem Solving,* by Barbara Minto, is

Reader-Friendly Style

Writing clear, content-driven sentences can be tough on people who want their writing to "flow." Think of it: the reason lullabies flow is that you are trying to get a child to fall asleep. Flowing sentences tend to be long, dense, and rhythmic. Choppy sentences are not better—too many of them can be distracting. Readers want the middle ground—brisk, hardworking sentences that carry good content. Brevity is not a virtue in business writing; conciseness is.

Reader-oriented business writing is also tough on people who think complex phrasing makes them look smarter. When a content-driven reader gets bogged

particularly helpful. An effective introduction, Minto says, briskly tells a story built around four elements:

1. THE SITUATION: A quick, factual sketch of the current business situation that serves to anchor the reader.

2. THE COMPLICATION: A problem that unsettles the situation in the story you're telling. It's why you're writing the memo or report.

3. THE QUESTION: This might be "What should we do?" "How can we do it?" or "What's wrong with what we tried?" The question does not necessarily have to be spelled out; it may be implied.

down in your phrasing, you don't look elegant or smart. You look pompous and self-absorbed.

Surprisingly, jargon—the specialized language of a particular field—is not inimical to good business writing, if it's suitable to your primary audience. Using jargon, like using acronyms, is a tight and efficient way to communicate among experts. But there are three situations in which you shouldn't use jargon: when it's meaningless, when you don't understand it, or when your readers aren't familiar with it. If you have multiple audiences and you want to use professional terminology because your primary audience uses it, define your term the first time you use it. For a long report, consider adding a glossary.

4. THE ANSWER: Your response to the question and your solution to the complication.

The order in which the elements appear can vary. Here are two examples:

Situation–Complication–Solution

(the question "What should we do?" is implicit)

Mediation's popularity has increased over the last quarter-century as people have sought alternative methods of dispute resolution that do not entail litigation's high cost and adversarial approach. But concern is growing that because mediators possess varying levels of training, the quality of mediation is unpredictable. I suggest that we use our organization's stature to spearhead a movement to professionalize the standards of practice for mediation so that mediators can get consistent, high-quality preparation in every state, and individuals or communities submitting to mediation will have confidence in their mediators' qualifications.

Question–Situation–Complication–Solution

What can we do to professionalize mediation so that the momentum gained over the last half-century is not lost? Individuals and communities turned to mediation in the first place to avoid the expense and conflict of litigation. But the increase in the number of mediators with varying levels of training makes the quality of mediation unpredictable, which causes dissatisfaction. I suggest that we use our organization's stature to spearhead a movement to establish standards of practice for mediation so that mediators can get high-quality training wherever they live, and individuals or communities submitting to mediation can have confidence in their mediators' qualifications.

Notice that shifting the order of the elements still satisfies the reader's expectation for the introduction. But it changes the tone, with the second example sounding more assertive.

Constructing the Pyramid

Now it's time to make the case for the solution you advocate. Minto has two recommendations. First, stay away from sentences initially and diagram your arguments and data as small, digestible chunks of information. Second, working from the top down, cluster and hang those chunks in a pyramid shape, with the information below developing and supporting the points above. An argument can travel horizontally across the chunks on its own level, but always in support of the chunk from which it hangs on the level above. Your thinking may have progressed from bottom up in the pyramid, but your writing is going to progress from top down.

Say you have just joined a midsize processed-food company. As the new vice president of business development, you are charged with identifying new markets and leading the creation of products for them.

Sales growth in the company's main product line, frozen dinners, has been stagnant for three years running. But you have identified a promising new target market: working parents between the ages of 35 and 55 who have sophisticated tastes and avoid preservatives and artificial ingredients. You want to convince your company's executive committee to create an upmarket line of organic frozen dinners with a Continental flair.

Some Final Tips

- PUT THE WEIGHT AT THE FRONT OF EACH SECTION. Readers like the journalistic approach—even if the story will break the hearts of millions, journalists give it away in the headline. But writers want to lead the reader, hand-in-hand, through their points and arguments to their conclusion. Except in murder mysteries, readers hate that.

- USE READER-ORIENTED JUDGMENT TO DECIDE THE RIGHT LEVEL OF DETAIL. Many overwriters pride themselves on their thoroughness, while underwriters congratulate themselves for being admirably brief. Both do a disservice to their readers and hence to themselves. Overwriters risk losing readers in a flood of detail, while underwriters may come across as superficial thinkers. From the reader's point of view, thorough means "exhaustive" and brief means "short"; the goal should be to be concise, which means "as tight as possible, but complete."

- REVISE BY PRINCIPLE; THERE IS NO TEMPLATE. Business writers beg for template sentences, but a template will distort a reader-oriented, content-driven memo or report every time.

The principles of good organization—fast, focused openings; the weight at the front of each section; a well-judged level of detail; and Minto's pyramid structure of logic—will serve you better than twisting your content to fit a generic template. Revising by principle will also help you more than the old standby advice: "Set it aside for 48 hours and come back to it." That's an effective way to give you a fresh eye for your writing, but when was the last time you had 48 hours to spare?

Reprint C0504C

Striking the Right Tone and Style

· · ·

When you select the right tone and style for your written communication, the document becomes even more effective. The selections in this section provide advice on ensuring the best possible match.

You'll learn the two qualities that determine tone—energy level and degree of formality—and find suggestions for controlling those qualities to strike the right tone for your piece. You'll also find suggestions for using style to connect emotionally with your readers; achieving a clear, compelling style; and fitting your style to the genre of the piece you're writing.

Find the Right Tone for Your Business Writing

• • •

Richard Bierck

Many writers agonize over word choice, syntax, and structure. But getting the words down on paper doesn't mean the job of writing is done. One of the most important steps in writing is matching the tone of the piece to the occasion—and the audience.

Tone in writing is an elusive quality that determines whether readers are put off or turned on, whether they laugh with you or at you, whether you come across as boor or a seer. Outlining a well-reasoned solution to a complex problem won't bring readers to your way of thinking unless the writing connects with them on a visceral level. Inappropriate tone leaves readers with a bad mental aftertaste. Appropriate tone allows the reader to concentrate on content without any background noise.

Most successful businesspeople have a keen sense of what's appropriate when talking to others. But many fail to apply this judgment to their writing—whether in e-mails, memoranda, letters, or proposals. Often, their writing is far too stiff and formal or too relaxed and colloquial. Just as often, writers produce pieces that are too upbeat for situations requiring more gravity, or too grave for circumstances calling for more energy.

For an appropriate tone in every circumstance, you need to carefully monitor two attributes—energy level and degree of formality.

Measure the energy conveyed in a piece of writing by asking, "How hot or cool should this memo be?" The extremes of the prose thermometer reveal the range of available choices. Here are examples of both polarities.

HOT: Anyone who hasn't had their head in the sand lately knows about the big problems we're having in the marketplace. Taking aim at the weaker items on our product line, a horde of well-trained competitors is inflicting mortal wounds. As a result, we are hemorrhaging revenues. How do we stanch the bleeding? Dump our weakest products and channel our energy into the stronger ones. That means we must pound out a powerful marketing plan to drive home the advantages of our products to the public. We must brainstorm ASAP to come up with a strategy that has teeth. If we fumble this one, we all may soon be standing in an unemployment line.

COOL: By now, most of us are probably aware of the critical challenges we're facing in the marketplace. Competitors are cutting into our market share and diminishing our revenues. The only solution may be to forgo some of our less successful products so that we may concentrate on the more successful. To do this, we'd have to streamline our marketing efforts to communicate value to consumers. This will require planning sessions to develop an effective strategy. I recommend that we proceed with all deliberate speed to develop a viable approach. The consequences of failing to move quickly and incisively could indeed be dire.

Though these two passages convey the same content and have the same intent—to motivate the reader to act— they vary greatly in tone. The hot passage draws on hyper- bole (the ostrich image), strong adjectives (e.g., "mortal"), and combat metaphors to communicate urgency. Strong verbs and vivid (at times, even surgical) images are used to incite the reader.

The cool passage is less alarming and, hence, conveys less urgency. It relies more on readers to discern the seri- ousness of the situation by reading between the lines a bit. While the tone of the hot passage is an alarmist call to action, that of the cool one is less likely to cause a panic, for it avoids emotionalism.

The second attribute to measure is formality. As with the energy level, the formality of a memo depends on the occasion, the recipient's predilections, and the character of the company.

You need to know what is right for your situation. In a venerable insurance company, for example, it's almost always better to stay well within the formal range of the spectrum. Conversely, if your company is a snowboard manufacturer, this kind of formality may only bring derision and consign your memo to the circular file.

Some examples:

INFORMAL: You've already got the 4-1-1 on what I'm going to say: Our sales figures reek. Competitors are putting the hurt on us in a serious way, and it's siphoning money out of your pocket and mine. The only way out of this mess may be to trash the losers in our product line and pump the winners. We're history unless we grease our marketing skids and persuade the public that using our products will produce euphoric moments. We must brainstorm ASAP to come up with a strategy that rocks. If we don't, we all may soon be asking: "You want fries with that?"

FORMAL: Only the myopic could now be unaware of our unfortunate position regarding market share.

Our sales figures have reached a nadir, and our competitors are getting the best of us, much to the detriment of our pocketbooks. Perhaps the only solution is to forgo the less profitable of our offerings, and focus our attention on our more successful products. Crucial to a recovery will be a well-crafted marketing program designed to heighten consumer demand. Failing to devise such a strategy may make all other concerns moot.

The informal passage is dominated by everyday colloquialisms. Instead of more lofty metaphors, it uses the slang of popular culture. Thirty years from now, readers would have a hard time understanding its meaning. Yet now, this tone can connect with certain kinds of audiences.

By contrast, the formal passage seeks no such personal connection and avoids common parlance. It distances the writer from his or her audience. While some readers might view this tone as being condescending, others would regard it as being appropriate for a specific business context.

In many ways, you'll find that the decisions surrounding energy and formality overlap. Informal compositions often tend to be hot or at least warm, but not always. Formal writing is typically cool, but it can sometimes include warm elements such as metaphor or short sentences that convey strong action.

Seldom do even professional writers achieve the

appropriate tone on the first draft. It takes a refined sensibility and careful honing. Even then, you may not be sure that you've struck the right tone.

To make sure, ask some people whose judgment you respect to give it a test read and get their reaction. Do they think it's too energetic or hyperbolic for the audience and the occasion? Or is it too frosty? Similarly, do they think the writing is too distant or too familiar? What are the offending words or phrases? How can they be changed to do the job at hand? Using test readers is hardly rocket science, but those willing to go to this trouble invariably produce more effective writing.

Using test readers may seem like a lot of trouble. But for writers committed to producing effective, impressive prose, this practice is less time-consuming than continuing to toil futilely in isolation. Test readers can help you get back on course before you've strayed too far.

And besides, it's good to share the agony of writing. In the end, however, writing remains a solitary sport, and you are ultimately responsible for developing the right content—as well as striking the right tone.

Reprint C0109D

Communication as a Change Tool

• • •

Stever Robbins

Tim Wallace knew he had a problem: customers were complaining about the delivery of built-to-order products and unhappy with his staff's lack of response. He knew a major change was needed but wasn't sure whether to start writing just another angry memo.

So Wallace decided instead to ask an unhappy customer to be videotaped, describing his experience with the company and his frustrations in asking for changes. The 15-minute video was eventually screened for 400 plant employees in a series of small meetings.

"A few mouths actually dropped open," Wallace recounts. "A minority was defensive. But just as many were saying, 'We've got to do something about this. We've got to do something.'"

Wallace's videotape became a catalyst that focused plant workers and managers on a problem that no one had been able to "get off the dime" to solve for years, he says. But the tape also was a classic illustration of the importance of communication in a change initiative, a key component experts say is often overlooked when leaders attempt to transform an organization.

"Change and communication go hand in hand," says Dan S. Cohen, who, with coauthor John P. Kotter, collected the stories of Wallace and other successful change leaders for their book *The Heart of Change*. "Yet too often I've heard leaders complain, 'I *said* this is what we're doing,' but then it still isn't happening.

"In the end, it's that communication and emotion"—the ability of employees to respond on a personal level—"that sustains the urgency to change. And it has to be recharged, again and again. Change isn't a 50-yard race, it's a marathon."

Cohen and other experts say that communicating this need and urgency is crucial for getting people behind a proposed change. Directives and memos from the top aren't enough: clear messages backed with concrete examples are needed for employees to focus and put their energies behind a new effort. The right messengers need to be on the front lines, reinforcing the ideas and providing the key link in the feedback loop. Most change efforts convey information about the desired change, but that's where most communication stops. Executives who want to make a lasting change in an organization need to have an ongoing conversation with the people who can tell them what is—and isn't—working every day.

Information Made Visible

"Organizations have complex, well-developed immune systems, aimed at preserving the status quo," write Peter Senge et al. in *The Dance of Change*. So leaders who want to launch a change initiative that will last have to first understand "how significant change invariably starts locally and how it grows over time," they say.

That's why showing small groups of employees the videotape of an unhappy customer complaining about faulty products and services has a far greater effect than a memo from the CEO outlining the need for "better customer relations." Not only did employees get an up-close look at the impact of the failure to remedy the situation, they were then immediately able to start talking about their own ideas regarding changes they could make to address the problem.

Similarly, Senge et al. cite the story of a nationwide plant maintenance initiative that was launched by a chemical company with great fanfare, only to sputter out after initially strong results. The management team had celebrated the success of its pilot program with a party and, confident that others in the company would want to learn from the experience, produced a booklet that described the new strategy. Yet even after the pilot was expanded to several other plants, the program failed once the first trainees moved on.

The team then regrouped and chose to narrow its focus. They zeroed in on pumps, which are trouble-prone yet crucial to overall production efficiency. They then further isolated their ten worst pumps. This focused effort grew to include 13 different locations. Although some plants still rejected the change, the programs that did take hold emboldened the management team to expand the effort to address larger maintenance challenges and overall plant operations. Starting with a smaller picture of change, the team concluded, was better.

In yet another example, Cohen and Kotter describe a purchasing manager who was trying to cut costs, without much success. So he quietly assembled an exhibit of work gloves, all purchased at wildly different prices from different vendors by his managers around the country. He

> Communication should be a two-way street from the moment a change initiative is announced.

piled the gloves on a table—revealing a *lot* of duplication—and invited his managers in for a visit. They quickly understood the problem.

These "visualizations," as Cohen and Kotter call them, provide the kind of dramatic confrontation with the facts that can convince employees of the need for change and remove some of the emotional blocks that reinforce the status quo.

A Pivotal Management Role

In his book *Real Change Leaders,* Jon R. Katzenbach writes that a frequently overlooked position on the organizational chart—the middle manager—can be crucial to a change initiative. Katzenbach says middle managers play such an important role because they are the ones who are directly responsible for improving performance through people.

These managers are the most plugged in to the concerns of employees and are the ones who will demonstrate daily the company's belief in the change effort. Without that kind of demonstration, cynical employees can easily shrug off the latest pronouncement from the CEO's office. Ignoring change directives became such an art at one manufacturer that employees even used the acronym AFP—"Another Fine Program"—for describing change initiatives.

"Too many leaders don't think through the implications, all the way down the line," says Cohen. "So when you and I hear about the change for the first time at some company announcement, there is no one to ask, 'What does this mean to me and my job?' In that sense, is the CEO really the most credible?"

Middle managers are key in communicating change because they are the people employees look to first to see if there is real acceptance of the idea, says Cohen. "Too many leaders don't realize that without the middle manager behind it, too many people think, 'I don't have to change. It's not going to happen anyway,'" says Cohen. "Too often the next level down says, 'Just let it go. If my boss doesn't tell me it is important, then it won't happen.'"

Because middle managers occupy such a central role, breaking down the communication plan to target them first in small sessions should be one of the cornerstones of a change initiative. But be prepared: middle managers, knowing they will hear the complaints and concerns of their unit employees, will be eager to ask questions and get details about job definitions, restructuring, compensation, and new policies.

Creating a Feedback Loop

Don't forget that communication should be a two-way street from the moment a change initiative is announced. When people help design new processes, they will be much more likely to use them. The more people contribute to answering the "how" questions, the more they will buy into making the "how" work.

In an aircraft company that Cohen surveyed, a new CEO was certain that he needed to quickly and definitively change how production problems were being handled. For senior management, he outlined the problem and what needed to happen in meetings.

But in order to reach frontline employees, the new leader spent time walking around the plant to talk to employees on the job. Instead of calling them to an auditorium, he found out where groups hung out, such as in the "smoking pit." He usually started by asking workers about the company and the problems they faced, and then he would ask for advice about the production problems that threatened to shut down the plant.

The weekly tour created a kind of automatic feedback program: when new ideas and steps were implemented, the CEO would be back within a few days to talk to workers about the changes, their reactions, and their suggestions for fine-tuning the process.

In another company, the CEO set up a weekly reporting program, where unit heads could collect questions and problems that the change initiative was running into. According to Cohen, this allowed him to use companywide meetings to confront the issues head on and measure what kind of misinformation was flowing around the change.

As positive change begins to emerge, it's just as important to remember that the feedback loop can also be a good way to celebrate successes, both large and small. If people don't notice the difference, point it out. Choose high-profile decisions that send a message throughout the organization. The more the new ways contrast with the old, the stronger that message will be.

For Further Reading

Real Change Leaders by Jon R. Katzenbach and the RCL Team (1997, Three Rivers Press)

The Heart of Change: Real-Life Stories of How People Change Their Organizations by John P. Kotter and Dan S. Cohen (2002, Harvard Business School Press)

The Dance of Change: The Challenges to Sustaining Momentum in Learning Organizations by Peter Senge et al. (1999, Currency Doubleday)

Reprint C0207C

Rhyme and Reason

What Poetry Has to Say
to Business Writers

• • •

Susan G. Parker

When Michael Henry started running poetry workshops, he expected to see a group of twentysomethings show up at his sessions at the Lighthouse Writers Workshop in Denver. To his surprise, most students were in their mid-forties and worked as lawyers, doctors, and corporate managers. To the students' surprise, the workshops turned out to improve their on-the-job communication.

"Writing poetry has improved my business writing," says Susan Bockhoff, a former manager of information technology for a medical manufacturing company. She signed up for the Lighthouse sessions, she says, "to do something creative."

"It helps you understand what people get from your writing," she says. "I'm now much more able to focus on the overall goal of my communication rather than getting mired in details that no one understands."

Transferable Discipline

Learning to write poetry can have a number of benefits for business writers, from learning to use the right metaphor to organizing a proposal to have maximum impact. That's because the focus and discipline needed to write poetry well can easily be transferred to improve any writing project, says Henry, codirector of the Lighthouse.

"Students learn to focus a poem by using clean language and specific detail so that the image is clear and the verbs are active, and they say, 'Wait a minute, I can use that in a memo.'"

> One benefit of writing and studying poetry is that it helps executives express complex ideas in simple words.

Mastering certain forms of poetry can also be good business writing discipline. Poetry is often written in certain forms, including haiku, sestina, or sonnet, which require facility with language and economy of expression. Likewise, business communications follow distinct forms, such as spreadsheets, reports, and memos, points out Mary Pinard, an English professor at Babson College who teaches MBA students and business executives to write poetry.

For some business executives, Pinard says, "the terror of making a poem is eased when using a form. There is a lot of discipline in writing poetry in closed forms. For some it is a comforting point of departure because they are used to working that way."

Conveying Complexity

Another benefit of writing and studying poetry is that it helps executives hone their ability to express complex ideas in simple words. In *Romeo and Juliet*, Juliet says, "What's in a name? That which we call a rose / By any other word would smell as sweet." This passage describes the abstract concept of naming in an engaging, concrete way, Henry points out.

The lessons Bockhoff learned from practicing the craft of poetry help her in her work as a consultant. She recently wrote a manual for a sales force that explained a new computer program.

> No more *stepping up to the plate, thinking outside the box,* or *leveraging.* Find strong, fresh images to make your point.

Instead of using off-putting jargon, she says, "I wrote it in real English. I got down to the guts of it, and the client loved it. Another thing I pay attention to is clichés. I absolutely can't stand those clichés anymore like *leverage* or *synergy* or *windows of opportunity.* They just make me want to gag. When people hear a cliché, their brain goes on autopilot because they've heard it so much from management. It doesn't mean anything. If you come up with something more honest and you're not just spouting off, people will pay more attention to what you're saying."

Susie Friedman is in product and business management at Quark, the publishing software company. She works daily with colleagues in the U.S., Europe, and India, and communicates mainly through e-mail. Friedman says that the poetry workshop helped her to develop new communication and problem-solving tactics that are particularly useful in more emotionally charged situations.

"I was having trouble getting an American and an Indian to listen to each other. Through the use of poetry, I was able to make the point about how important listening and taking the time to understand another's point of view was," she says. "I used poetry to help someone pause rather than continue to bash away on a point."

Pinard tells the story of an insurance executive who became so enthusiastic after one of her executive courses that he spent the plane ride back home writing poems. He now spends time most days writing poetry, sometimes alone and sometimes with employees, she says.

Poetry instructors offer these seven tips for honing your business writing:

Just get it down.

Write a first draft, and understand that you will write another and perhaps another. "Most good poets understand that the first draft of any poem that they write is lousy," Henry says. "But they have to get the first draft out there. A lot of business writers are paralyzed writers. They sit down and look at the screen. They get stuck, they put it off, and this increases their stress level.

"Creative writers," he continues, "especially poets, understand that the most important thing is to put it down on the page. It gives you something to work with. Then you edit."

Use the active voice.

Using the passive voice is a way to avoid responsibility. "A lot of times business writing values the passive, like '$14 million was lost,'" Henry says. "While people who are writing in business may feel a pressure to obfuscate, they are not getting their message across. You have to own up to it. People see you as a more honest person when you do. They will want to work for you more."

Avoid clichés at all costs.

No more *stepping up to the plate, thinking outside the box,* or *leveraging.* Find strong, fresh images to make your point. Henry applauds this passage from IBM's 2000 annual report, which talks about the dot-com crash:

> That's not the way things seemed a year ago. Back then, it looked as though Internet start-ups were taking over and traditional bricks-and-mortar enterprises had better jump with both feet into "e-tailing" or get steamrolled.

> "*Bricks-and-mortar, jump with both feet,* and *steamrolled:* All interesting and clear images in figurative language that is not clichéd," he says.

Vary the length of your sentences.

"Good business writing should be conversational," says Mark Gelade, a San Francisco writer who teaches a class for businesses called Poets in the Workplace. "You can hear the rhythm of the language. Language that is highly readable has a lot of variety in the length of the sentences. A good mix of long and short sentences is pleasing to the ear."

Use the fewest words possible.

"It comes down to checking your language for any word that is not pulling its weight," Gelade says. "You have to go on a hunting expedition for words that are superfluous."

Henry's advice: "Simplify. Break those long sentences with lots of clauses into three or four sentences. It gives the language more vibrancy. It saves the reader time and energy. If your message is unclear, people get frustrated."

Read your writing out loud.

Reading something you have written aloud—or at least mouthing the words—can help you spot flaws in it that you'd otherwise miss. Such problems as repetition, ambiguity, faulty transitions, and awkward phrasing will jump out at you when you hear them—and when you hear yourself struggling to read the passages in which they occur.

Read poetry.

Poetry is more accessible than many people may think. Modern and contemporary poets like Billy Collins, Elizabeth Bishop, Mark Strand, and Jane Kenyon, to name just a few, write poems that tell stories. They do so in a compact, lyrical way that draws the reader in. Anthologies, such as *Good Poems,* collected by Garrison Keillor, or *Americans' Favorite Poems,* coedited by former U.S. Poet Laureate Robert Pinsky, offer an array of poems to sample. The Pinsky volume includes comments from readers, including business executives, about how the poems affected them.

"The most common myth about poetry is that it is intended for the culturally elite," Gelade says. "The more I study and read Shakespeare, the more apparent it is that it is much more like *Pulp Fiction* than an academic thesis. The biggest preconception people have is that they can't write poetry. It's a very good thing as an adult to challenge yourself to do things that you may not have thought you could do."

For Further Reading

Good Poems, Garrison Keillor, ed. (2002, Viking)

Americans' Favorite Poems: The Favorite Poem Project Anthology, Robert Pinsky and Maggie Dietz, eds. (1999, W.W. Norton)

Reprint C0305D

Ayn Rand
on Writing

• • •

Theodore Kinni

"Writing is something one can learn," declared Ayn Rand. "There is no mystery about it." In 1969, over 16 evenings, the novelist-philosopher demystified writing in a series of informal lectures given to a small group of colleagues. Her lectures were taped, and, 19 years after her death in 1982, edited and published as *The Art of Nonfiction*.

Although best known for her two perennially popular novels of ideas, *The Fountainhead* (1943) and *Atlas Shrugged* (1957), Rand devoted her later life almost exclusively to nonfiction, promulgating her philosophy of Objectivism through speeches, essays, and articles. Objectivism was and remains controversial, but Rand made sure that it was always clearly and compellingly presented.

For all her success, Rand was not a born writer, at least not in English. She spoke the language only haltingly and did not yet write it when, at age 20, she left Communist Russia for the United States in 1926. It took her years to master writing in her adopted language, and throughout her career she worked hard to improve her craft.

The three most important elements of effective nonfiction writing, said Rand, are "*clarity, clarity,* and *clarity.*" Beyond that, she believed in writing first from the subconscious, without the interference of the conscious mind. Once the first draft is down on paper, then editing can begin. Following are her tips for writing as clearly and powerfully as Rand herself.

Limit Subject and Theme

Rand advised writers to answer three questions at the start of any project:

- WHAT WILL I WRITE ABOUT? Define the topic and be sure that you can cover it adequately within the parameters of the project.

- WHAT DO I WANT TO SAY ABOUT THIS SUBJECT? Determine the theme of your project—the point of view that you want to communicate.

- IS WHAT I HAVE TO SAY NEW? If not, then don't put pen to paper at all, advised Rand.

Judge the Audience

Most of us, and certainly all business writers, are writing to an audience. So, in order to write persuasively, we need to identify the characteristics of our intended audience.

Create a Plan of Action

Like many experienced writers, Rand was a firm believer in the power of the outline and suggested two tests to measure an outline's completeness. The first is the essence test: an outline is complete only when you can understand it as a unified whole. "If the abstract structure is not clear in your mind, you cannot hold in mind the overall view of your [project] or decide what belongs in it," said Rand, "so problems will arise."

The second is the test of final causality. This test, which Rand adapted from Aristotelian philosophy, says that when your outline establishes and details a logical chain of cause-and-effect steps that lead to the established conclusion, it is complete.

Draft from the Subconscious

Rand believed in the creativity of the human subconscious. "While you are writing," she said, "you must adopt the premise: my subconscious, right or wrong." Rand suggested that you write without stopping and to the greatest extent possible, without consciously thinking out each sentence. Don't slip into editing or make major changes in the draft, and try to work in complete sequences. All of this, said Rand, will allow you to maximize the output of your subconscious mind and minimize your need to edit.

Edit Objectively

Rand proposed a three-level approach to editing.

First, focus on the structure of the work. At this level, you need to ensure that it progresses logically and respects the reader's intelligence.

Second, focus on clarity. Ensure that the writing is communicating exactly what you intend it to. Rand warns writers to beware of *overcondensing*—cramming too much into a sentence or paragraph—and *automatization*—a rote sequence in their own thinking that assumes too much of the reader.

Third, consider style. Her tips:

- Don't complicate a simple thought.

- The simpler the words, the better.

- Don't use sarcasm, pejorative adjectives, or inappropriate humor.

- Don't use bromides.

- Don't use unnecessary synonyms.

For Further Reading

The Art of Nonfiction: A Guide for Writers and Readers by Ayn Rand; ed., Robert Mayhew (2001, Plume)

Reprint C0301C

When One Style Does Not Fit All

• • •

John Clayton

So you've finally been given the go-ahead to develop that pet project of yours. You're convinced it could not only be a success, but save the company, which has been turning out either flat or slightly negative earnings for the past several quarters. Your idea—a potentially very profitable niche product—can be run on downtime in an existing plant, so the risk is very small.

All the signs look good. There's only one thing standing between you and all that glory: the proposal.

You've written 20 drafts and none of them gets it right. You've considered the audience—first your manager,

> The more you understand the underlying logic and purpose of the genre, the more effectively you can use it.

then the divisional VP, and then, if all goes well, the board. Your manager is a meat-and-potatoes guy who just wants the facts, as briefly as possible. The divisional VP is more of a holistic thinker; she likes a context wrapped around the proposal. You have no idea what the board will respond to, but you suspect it has a lot to do with how the VP presents it, so she's your real hurdle.

You've thought about all this, but something's still missing. These people read dozens of proposals each month. How can yours stand out? How can you convince them that this one is the special one that deserves a green light?

You need to think through the *genre* you're writing in.

"A genre isn't just mystery, science fiction, or romance," says Anne Beaufort, author of *Writing in the Real World*. "Every recurring form has conventions." Whether you're writing a proposal, press release, status memo, or lab report, chances are it fits into a genre. The faster you can pin down the genre and its conventions, the more quickly and effectively you can write. Then the secret becomes fulfilling the generic expectations fully enough to show that you're savvy and violating them enough to show that you can stand out from the crowd. It's one of the most difficult writing challenges to get right.

Beaufort followed four employees for a year as they performed writing tasks in their jobs at a nonprofit job service agency. She found that most of her subjects' writing fit into one of five or six genres, such as internal memos, letters to customers, proposals, or press releases. The genre defined the most basic qualities of the document:

RHETORICAL FEATURES. Each genre addresses the audience's expectations and needs in a particular way. For example, in the genre of meeting minutes, the audience expects written documentation of what happened at the meeting—more specifically, a summary of the decisions that were made. The audience needs this information to stay up to date on organizational strategy; its expectations thus differ from customers needing product information or suppliers needing specs. For your new product proposal, the genre calls for establishing right at the start what the stakes are, and what the potential benefits are to the company—all in a couple of sentences. Think of that opening as sufficient reason for a busy VP to read further.

CONTENT. For example, a new project proposal needs to contain the opener, a longer section describing the essence of the new product, a section spelling out the demands the new product will place on the organization, including cost and profit analyses, and a final section that puts the product in the larger context of the company's goals and mission. In contrast, meeting minutes contain summaries of topics discussed at a meeting. A newly won contract, a new dress code, or a new hire—no matter how important to this audience—should not be included in meeting minutes if they were not discussed at the meeting.

STRUCTURE. For each type of document, there are guidelines for organizing information. A product proposal, for example, must follow the thought processes of the busy executive. Each section, therefore, needs to be clearly labeled and set apart from the others. Consider giving your executive a chance to give the proposal a 30-second look, a two-minute look, and a thorough going-over that might last 30 minutes. If the executive needs more detail than that, it's probably better for her to meet with you or your team in person.

STYLISTIC ELEMENTS. Here you must decide on the appropriate language, use of jargon, formatting, etc. For example, memos follow a specific heading format, with lines indicating who the memo is from, to whom it's addressed, the date, and the subject matter. Additionally, memos generally go to people who are at least somewhat familiar with the issues and thus may contain less background, and more acronyms, than documents in different genres that cover the same topics. With business proposals, jargon should be kept to a minimum—but not eliminated entirely. Used judiciously, jargon is a code that signals to the reader that you are expert in this particular field of endeavor. It should be linked with simple, clear phrasing and active verbs.

In the book *Genre Analysis,* John M. Swales notes that as a trendy synonym for classification, "genre" is now applied to things such as music videos, presidential press conferences, game shows, and large floppy rag dolls. But in the specific sense of a recurring form of communication with specialized purposes, the genre deserves attention because it both establishes rhetorical goals and furthers

> Regardless of genre, you owe your readers certain basic qualities of good writing: clarity, brevity, and white space.

their accomplishment. For example, the genre of the résumé has well-defined goals (primarily to acquire work); it also has well-defined structural, organizational, formatting, and linguistic standards that have developed because they are the best way to achieve those goals.

How do you recognize a genre? Swales suggests the following criteria:

A GENRE IS A COMMUNICATION EVENT WITHIN A SPECIFIC ENVIRONMENT. It may be quite common and mundane (a supermarket checkout encounter) or rare and important (a papal encyclical). The audience may be narrow or large—but as the phrase "communication event" implies, we're looking not at a document or presentation but at the process of getting a message across to a specific audience. The tricky aspect of our proposal on the new product is that there are really three communication events involved: reaching the manager, the VP, and ultimately the board. It is quite possible that you will need three slightly different proposals for each "event."

THE GENRE HAS A SPECIFIC PURPOSE OR SET OF PURPOSES. Your press release about the company's new vice president for governmental affairs primarily brags about the new hire. But additional purposes may be to mold public opinion and/or hint at a legislative agenda for the coming year. It pays to think in sophisticated ways about what those purposes might be. For example, with the product proposal, you want your product to make money for the company. But what about divisional competition? How important is that in your company? Should you subtly stress that, or should its appeal be blatant? Or are there company rules against interdivisional competition?

THESE PURPOSES SHAPE A GENRE'S STRUCTURE, CONTENT, AND STYLE. For example, Swales compares the *good-news letter* ("I'm happy to offer you the job . . .") and the *bad-news letter* ("I regret to inform you that your application was rejected by the committee . . ."). One purpose of the good-news letter is to get you to respond rapidly and positively; thus it's personal and emotional. Conversely, the impersonal, unemotional bad-news letter is designed to signal that communications have ended. Proposals are fundamentally about pushing a bureaucracy to take a chance on trying something new—always a painful prospect. The incentive is that the bureaucracy may make money from the opportunity.

The audience may not be fully conscious of all of these purposes. Indeed, even the writer—especially the novice writer—may not understand all that a genre accomplishes. This last feature is why it's best to follow established genre formats—mostly. You need to reserve the crucial element of surprise in order to get your piece to stand out. But these formats have evolved an underlying logic and rationale over years of serving the genre's purposes. The more you can understand the underlying logic and purpose of the genre, the more effectively you can use it, says Beaufort. A grant writer she interviewed talked about his struggles with government grant-writing procedures until he understood the "deep purposes" of the genre in the context of government funding agencies' agendas.

Experts allow the genre concept a good deal of fuzziness—for example, nobody wants to debate whether a new-product announcement for the industry press is a different genre than one for the consumer press. The point is that most types of documents follow conventions to achieve their goals. Those who regularly use the genre know the conventions intimately, if sometimes subconsciously. And the easiest way for novice writers to pick up on these conventions is to follow examples at first. Once you know the genre inside and out, it's time to begin experimenting—very carefully. The ultimate key to success is to fulfill the basic expectations and then go beyond them in one or two specific, calculated ways. A corollary rule is not to venture into a new genre for the first time when the stakes are too high. Don't make your critical product proposal the first one you've ever done. If you're a neophyte, get help from someone who knows the ropes, or at least study examples of previously successful proposals.

The only danger in this last approach comes if the

examples are not up to snuff. As communication consultant Lee Clark Johns points out in her article "The File Cabinet Has a Sex Life: Insights of a Professional Writing Consultant," blindly mimicking what you find in the file cabinet can merely repeat the mistakes of the past, and thus fail to meet your readers' needs.

Regardless of genre, Johns believes, you owe your readers certain basic qualities of good writing: clarity, brevity, and white space. You also owe them a structure with conclusions stated clearly at the beginning—this is an essential aspect of writing for the business world, where readers are impatient and need to know what's in it for them right from the start.

She also objects to many corporate documents' "pedantic style," featuring long sentences, passive verbs, and a too-formal vocabulary. Unfortunately, some writers (especially young or insecure ones) think this style sounds professional. Yet, she says, "I know of no corporate executive who says, 'Impress me with big words and long sentences.' I know of many who complain about the complexity of the documents they must read."

When you become experienced with a genre, you can consider altering its conventions. This may be especially true for managers who are instructing others what (and how) to write. You are familiar with the genre's audience, with its multiple purposes, and with what you yourself want to read. Now is the time to see if the examples in the file cabinet fulfill the objectives of the genre.

Beaufort says that as she followed writers around in their jobs, she found a similar phenomenon. She asked Birgit, a now-seasoned grant writer who knows the job-service agency grant proposal genre well, to look again at some of the early grants she had written for the organization. Birgit's response: "No wonder I didn't get that grant! Look at what I did!" In hindsight, Birgit could see the way she'd violated the genre's conventions.

The story illustrates Beaufort's key recommendation to businesspeople seeking to improve their writing: become a *self-reflective* writer. She suggests you keep files of what you've written—perhaps several files for several genres—and periodically review them for the writing. How does each meet or break genre standards? How have those decisions met (or failed to meet) readers' needs? What was the result of each communiqué? Did it accomplish the result you wanted? Did it have to go through multiple drafts and revisions? What can "failed" documents tell you about your audience's needs?

Becoming a self-reflective writer is a responsibility you have to take for yourself. In fact, a manager may not even give you feedback on your writing. The manager is interested in results: wooing the customer, getting the proposal approved, swaying the public. How did what you wrote produce those results (or fail to produce them)? That's the question your own genre analysis can help answer.

For Further Reading

Writing in the Real World: Making the Transition from School to Work by Anne Beaufort (1999, Teachers College Press)

Genre Analysis: English in Academic and Research Settings by John M. Swales (1990, Cambridge University Press)

"The File Cabinet Has a Sex Life: Insights of a Professional Writing Consultant" by Lee Clark Johns in *Strategies for Business and Technical Writing*, 4th ed., edited by Kevin J. Harty (1999, Allyn & Bacon)

Reprint C0202E

Surmounting Special Writing Challenges

· · ·

In an age marked by increasing use of e-mail, economies fueled by high technology, and mounting pressure to quickly absorb and act on the content of written communications, all managers face new challenges in the writing tasks they undertake. The articles in this section help you tackle the most daunting of these challenges.

You'll discover strategies not only for writing effective e-mails but also for helping yourself and your direct reports translate highly technical ideas into persuasive, accessible language for readers who lack a technical background. Additional selections focus on how to write an effective executive summary and how to ensure that a written piece follows length restrictions.

Don't Push That Send Button!

• • •

Nick Morgan

In 1999, *Harvard Management Communication Letter* ran an article boldly setting forth what we called "The Ten Commandments of E-mail." The piece attracted a good deal of healthy commentary about the role of this new form of communication in corporate life. It's about time to look back and see which commandments still make sense and which need revision—and whether any new ones are necessary.

Today, we are all much more proficient in the use of e-mail. Generational reluctance to use e-mail has faded away; indeed, in 2001 seniors comprised the fastest-growing user segment. And yet, some of our bad habits have persisted, and a few new problems have emerged since the original piece ran.

The most important problem in 1999 was the already overwhelming overload of information, which was exacerbated by the widespread adoption of e-mail. E-mail is what the experts call a nearly "frictionless" form of communication, which means it's easy to do—you don't have to go to a post office or even find a stamp. Just push a button, and you can blanket the world with your thoughts.

Today, that situation has become entrenched. Nearly every modern corporate citizen is now on e-mail and has to deal with a vast amount of associated junk. In addition to junk e-mail, we now have pop-up ads and other forms of online irritation that slow down the daily chore of separating the useful information from the trash.

How can we deal with this even more acute crisis? Douglas Neal, a research fellow at CSC Research Services, advocates taking an active stance in controlling your e-mail flow, particularly with regard to educating your colleagues to use e-mail wisely. He says, "The point is that you have to take actions, not just be passive. You have to reward those who do good and explain to those who are doing wrong that they have done so. Don't get mad, get it changed! Those who suffer quietly will continue to suffer!"

Neal recommends a two-step process for coping with your e-mail. First, he says, analyze the e-mail you receive, charting whether it's useful or not and how often you get both kinds. Then, tactfully tell those who regularly send you lots of low-utility e-mail to stop doing so. Neal points out that overload is in the eye of the recipient: some are overwhelmed by 10 e-mails a day, whereas others can easily handle 100. Take a week or so to chart your incoming e-mail. Then you can organize it with an eye toward addressing any problems that the analysis brings to light.

In the short run, HMCL still recommends performing daily "triage" on your e-mail inbox. Scan the entire list, eliminating all the junk mail first. Then group the remaining mail by action needed, just as you would a real inbox on your desk. The efficiency experts tell us that you should handle paper only once in an office, deciding when you first look at it whether to discard it, keep it for filing, or place it on the "do list." You can manage your e-mail overload in the same way.

Beyond the overload issue, the commandments we brought back from the digital mountain in 1999 identified some other times you might want to think twice about hitting "send." (We've rephrased some of them slightly for today's more sophisticated e-mail users.)

Use e-mail only when it's the most efficient channel for your need.

Three years ago, we said, "What most people seem to forget is that it's e-*mail*. It's really a modern form of something

> Even your deleted e-mails can be resurrected and read in courtrooms by lawyers who are not friends of yours.

your great-grandparents used: the letter. The modern incarnation is best for short, informal messages that need to be both written and read. Messages that don't fall into that category might be better handled in a different way."

This was very good advice then, and it remains good advice. In fact, we now have even more options in our grab bag of communication channels: instant messages, text messaging, chat rooms, and even pager code for the teenage crowd.

Each of these other channels is faster, more immediate, and—this is key—more perishable than e-mail. E-mail is forever, and therein lies the rub. When you need to commit something to print, use e-mail. In the business world, that list of needs should be confined to concrete requests, queries, and responses. In other words, the bare-bones daily details of work.

For gossip, back chat, networking, water cooler exchanges, and all those other delightful aspects of business wheel-greasing, use the telephone or one of the other digital forms, where the record is less complete. Or even a face-to-face meeting! (More about this later.)

For messages with a greater feeling of permanence, or more punch, consider writing a real letter, on nice stationery, signed and dated by hand, and mailed through the post. You'd be surprised at how great a personal impact a traditional letter can have in this era of digital impermanence.

Never print your e-mail.

This commandment has not stood up as well over time. We were trying to bring about the paperless office and save trees. But because of the litigious nature of our society, you may well want to keep printed copies of e-mail you've sent as well as e-mail sent to you. Of course, as we've all learned, even e-mail that's been deleted can be recovered, but why take a chance? Print it and take a minute to lament the undeniable fact that the paperless office won't arrive any time soon.

Tony DiRomualdo, strategy and IT researcher, says, "We should not forget that e-mail is a very powerful and persistent medium that poses real and significant risks to companies. Surely the Andersen/Enron scandal holds many lessons about this point. And if used for the wrong purposes it can have nasty consequences. Don't say anything you would not want the entire planet to read at some point." But if you insist on saying something potentially actionable, keep a copy for your own records.

Send nothing over e-mail that must be error-free.

Time has only strengthened our opinion that this commandment is right on target. We said then, "It is simply impossible to proofread successfully on the computer screen." That is just as true now as it was then. If a communication must be error-free, then print it out, pick up something like an old-fashioned ruler, and read away, slowly, line by line. Then reread it backwards, word by word. And remember that spell checkers don't catch the wrong word spelled correctly. Get someone else to read your words, too.

Never delete names from your address book.

This advice remains especially pertinent for the virtually challenged. And yet it hardly seems like the biggest challenge we face today in the virtual world. It will save time to keep an up-to-date address book and to know how to use it. But not much time, unless you're prone to sending out a good many broadcast e-mails. And why would you want to do that? That usually comes under the heading of "spam," and it's at the heart of the problem of information overload.

Never forward chain e-mail.

In the past several years, there has been no lessening of this scourge! It is a practice universally decried, and yet we all know people who do it—and most of us will admit to having perpetrated a chain e-mail ourselves late on a Friday when everyone else has left early and we're still stuck in the office.

Never send e-mail when you're furious or exhausted.

This is even better advice than we knew at the time. Look at Microsoft, for example. The e-mails key players sent got them their day in court, and it wasn't what they wanted. It's an example we all can learn from. Legally, e-mail belongs to the company that provides the system and the link-up. You don't have privacy as an individual. And the court can wrest the e-mail records from the company, as happened to Microsoft. Don't—*don't*—commit anything to writing you wouldn't want to have read in court. Period.

Don't pass on rumor or innuendo about real people.

We repeat this advice in recalling the British man who boasted about his sexual exploits of the night before in an e-mail, only to see the boast spread out to thousands of e-mail recipients in a matter of hours. Avoid spreading false information about real, live people. It will come back to haunt you. Even your deleted e-mails can be resurrected and read in courtrooms by lawyers who are not friends of yours.

Nor should you do so about companies you work for or may work for one day.

In the intervening years, this practice has grown up and become a Web site. Most companies have at least one rogue site that mocks them, slanders them, or disses their products. Apparently, this advice pertains only to a distant, more civilized era—say, 1999. And these Web sites sure are handy when you're considering a job offer from a company that has one.

Never substitute e-mail for a necessary face-to-face meeting.

Anecdotal evidence of layoffs accomplished via e-mail only serves to reinforce this point. Here's what we said then, and every manager should have these sentences bronzed and placed in a conspicuous place in the office: "Never reprimand, reward, or fire someone who reports to you via e-mail. There's a special circle of hell awaiting those who do. We owe it to our humanity to perform these obligations, whether difficult or easy, in person. And remember that when you're trying to persuade someone to do something, or someone wants to persuade you, there is no substitute for a face-to-face meeting."

Remember this hierarchy: first the meeting, then the phone call, then the voice mail, then the e-mail.

This commandment still holds true: for the greatest impact, hold a meeting. You get more "bandwidth" face to face. The phone call eliminates the body language, but maintains tone and live exchange. Voice mail gets tone but does without live exchange. And an e-mail is neither live nor terribly nuanced. Hence the frequent misunderstandings about jokes attempted over e-mail, and those annoying but necessary little dingbats people use to signal emotion.

Final score: 80% of the Ten Commandments of e-mail still hold true. Some 20% have not held up or are now irrelevant. What about advice we would give now that we didn't then? Just one, our eleventh commandment:

Your e-mail is hackable and retrievable, and it can be used against you. Use only when absolutely necessary.

E-mail is an extremely efficient form of communication when used sensibly—but be careful out there. It's a litigator's paradise.

Reprint C0208E

How to Engineer Compelling Prose

Teaching a Techie to Write

• • •

John Clayton

An engineer, the old joke goes, is the type of person who would rather take a telephone apart than use it to call his mother. This bit of humor actually reveals a truism of the engineering world: sometimes, engineers' close attention to how an object works causes them to overlook the object's larger relevancy.

This focus on analysis and understanding helps the engineer in his job, but it can stymie you in yours as his manager. Say you want to make a compelling case for a bigger chunk of company resources. If the technical members of your staff can't persuasively articulate how their proposed projects will translate into bottom-line business payoffs, your bid is going to be dead in the water.

Fortunately, there are strategies you can employ to help engineers and other technically inclined types on your staff create clear, cogent prose.

Why They Write That Way

Engineers' personalities and education deserve credit for work that has greatly improved our lives. Their accomplishments have come largely from manipulating *things*. Thus, to them, the object is paramount, says professor Daniel Ding of Ferris State University, who specializes in technical and science writing. It's what they work with, design, and control. Engineers' language naturally reflects such concerns, which can lead them to construct wordy, noun-filled, passive-voice sentences such as "The 10-32 1¾ inch wood screw was driven into the hickory with a Phillips head screwdriver 5¾ revolutions."

Moreover, engineers tend to organize their thoughts around their understanding of a system. But their nonengineer peers and managers care less about the objects that make up a system and how the system works than they do about what that system as a whole can help them accomplish.

Engineers also are often reluctant to try to convey ideas to those outside their field because they are unsure how to communicate with those who lack specialized knowledge. "We all stay within a comfort zone," notes Barbara Bryan, a trained engineer and independent business writer. "With engineers, that means they may have little experience talking plain English to everyday people."

Thus engineers have a difficult time understanding how to write for other audiences, says Ron Tulley, who teaches writing to engineering students at Case Western Reserve University. "There's a vast difference in expertise between engineers and any other audience. And they have a big fear of 'dumbing down.'"

As well, some engineers and other technical specialists are uncomfortable working in what they perceive as the subjective field of writing. Technical work is a complex, highly rules-based enterprise. Writing well is also a complicated endeavor but one whose rules are decidedly less absolute. Thus engineers, accustomed to their cut-and-dried world, hesitate to labor in a less objective discipline.

Improving Engineers' Communication

To advance their business unit and further their careers, technical types sometimes have to communicate their specialized knowledge to a nontechnical audience. Here are four ways that a manager can help them do this:

> ## To communicate better with engineers, adopt some of their language.

1. Define the audience's needs for them.

"Engineers face the same problem as all of us," says Paul Anderson, director of the Center for Writing Excellence at Miami University of Ohio. "How do we talk about what we do in ways that are useful to others?" Engineers are used to answering questions from other engineers, but managers typically ask questions that serve different needs. So you must articulate those different needs. Once engineers understand what a reader wants, Anderson says, they find constructing individual sentences easier.

For example, say a metallurgist at an auto company has been researching why a prototype's piston rod continues to break. She may be tempted to present her results as if she were addressing an audience of other metallurgists, using specific terminology and framing her results to satisfy the questions other specialists in her field might have.

But discussing the piston rod's metallurgic properties won't help design engineers, who seek information about redesigning the system, nor would doing so aid managers, who want to know how long the problem will take to fix and which processes will be affected.

The more managers can identify which questions need to be answered, Anderson says, the more successfully engineers can rise to the challenge on their own terms. "Focus on usability, not readability," he says. Engineers are more familiar with the concept of how readers can use documents than they are with what seems to them the vague concept of readability.

How do you make readers' needs more concrete? You might try creating a representative reader, one you describe in detail. Alan Cooper, author of *The Inmates Are Running the Asylum: Why High-Tech Products Drive Us Crazy and How to Restore the Sanity,* suggests introducing engineers to a persona—a hypothetical but specific audience member. Since engineers love the tangible, he advises using specifics, including a name and a face, to make that pretend individual distinct. "For example, we don't just say that Emilee uses business software. We say that Emilee uses WordPerfect Version 5.1 to write letters to Gramma . . . [and drives] a dark-blue 1991 Toyota Camry with a gray plastic kid's seat strapped into the back and an ugly scrape on the rear bumper."

2. Probe.

When technical specialists are uncomfortable addressing nontechnical audiences, sit down with them and ask the types of questions that will elicit the responses you're looking for. "I keep asking questions to get them down to the appropriate level," says Bryan. "What's the assumption under that? How did you get from point A to point B? Will your audience understand that word?"

Case Western Reserve's Tulley agrees. "Interaction with others is the only way" to help engineers reach beyond their disciplines, he says. "It's just practice, practice, practice."

3. Help them structure the document.

When Bryan edits engineers' reports, she says, "I usually have to reorganize." A need to restructure often results because the writer did not use any sort of an outline. (Or he wrote the outline as a last step.) For instance, factual information may appear in the "Recommendations" section, or vice versa. Bryan finds this problem ironic. "The same engineer who mixes up parts of a report on a ground water study wouldn't dream of completing the steps of the study haphazardly," she says.

A manager can help a technical specialist structure his writing by providing an outline or a sample document that serves as a template. The writer can use such a concrete, tangible model in much the same way as he uses a set of formulas or follows certain rules, knowing that they work because they're proven.

Managers also can increase their effectiveness in communicating with engineers by adopting some of their language. What if, when handing over that outline, you called it a flow chart? Most engineers are familiar with flow charts, which detail the steps they need to take to move from an initial state to a desired outcome. In essence, that's what an outline does. So why not frame it as such?

4. Help them edit and format their work.

You can help technical types achieve strong, unambiguous writing by working with them to eliminate jargon and edit unclear sentences. The first draft of a report may contain too much technical language and too many passive-voice constructions, as well as too few and/or too many disclaimers. That doesn't mean the report's ideas are not sound.

Simple rules exist on how to eliminate the passive voice, for example, or how to substitute smaller words for bigger ones. Furthermore, computerized word-processing tools, while far from perfect, allow such rules to be applied quickly and comprehensively. But this is best done after the rough draft is complete—there's no need to get the writer bogged in too many details until she has got something down on paper.

Once the document is nearly complete, help the writer format it so that its information is more accessible. Highlighting the most important ideas with headings, lists, and boldface can help drive home the points that you want the document to make. An added bonus is that such formatting can distract from weak supporting prose.

For Further Reading

Technical Communication: A Reader-Centered Approach by Paul V. Anderson (2003, Heinle)

Reprint C0407D

Writing an Executive Summary That Means Business

• • •

John Clayton

Responding to a request for proposals (RFP) is pretty straightforward. You describe your company's history, your product or service, its implementation schedule, and the support you'll provide. The one stumbling block is the one section that everyone will read: the executive summary.

What is its purpose? If you answered, *to summarize the proposal,* think again.

"*Executive summary* is a bit of a misnomer," says Tom Sant, founder of Sant Corporation and author of *Persuasive Business Proposals: Writing to Win Customers, Clients, and Contracts.* "What you're really trying to do is lay out the business case."

Thus the executive summary demands a whole different approach to writing than the rest of the proposal, one that balances efficient delivery of key information with a persuasive, well-substantiated pitch. Above all, the executive summary must demonstrate a clear understanding of the potential client's needs. A good way to do this is to include in it the ROI your services will deliver. "You need to describe outcomes," Sant says. "Describe the impact on performance—ideally a measurable impact."

Write with an Eye to the Audience

A strong executive summary is crafted with the audience firmly in mind: busy executives interested in bottom-line deliverables, not details. "An executive reads for certain keywords, and for the price," says Stacia Kelly, president of Catklaw, a writing boutique. "If he likes it, he'll hand it to an assistant and ask them to read the whole thing."

For that reason, advises Bud Porter-Roth, author of *Proposal Development: How to Respond and Win the Bid,* put the most critical information in the first couple of paragraphs. "The executive may not read any more," he says. But, he cautions, "the RFP writers will read the whole thing." Thus the executive summary has an additional, secondary audience: the middle managers who will make presentations about you and your proposal to senior management. So make sure the executive summary gives them the tools to act on your behalf, Porter-Roth says. To reach both of these audiences, an executive summary should do three things:

1. Establish the need or problem.

This might be more challenging than first appears. Often, says Porter-Roth, "RFPs are poorly written. You may have to define the business issues, because the RFP was written by technical people who saw only technical issues."

"You need to convince them that this is a problem worth doing something about," Sant says. "Your biggest competitor may be that they do nothing, that they spend this money on something else."

2. Recommend the solution and explain its value.

"Be sure to make a firm, clear recommendation," advises Sant. For example, say something along the lines of "We recommend that integrated content management software be implemented across the company." Then you need to explain the value of your solution. Here you're not focusing on what it is, but on what its return or benefits will be.

"Rather than technical details, you need to say things

like 'This solution will reduce your work staff by five people' or 'This CRM will allow you to answer questions while on line, rather than in a call back,'" says Porter-Roth.

3. Provide substantiation.

Give the key reasons why your company is the right company to deliver the solution. Here's where you can differentiate yourself—highlight a unique methodology, for instance, or provide a quick case study of your past work. Another idea: Include testimonials from satisfied clients. Just don't get carried away and turn the focus away from the potential client and onto your company. "It's not about the vendor—it's about the customer," says Sant. His rule of thumb: Make sure the executive summary mentions the customer's name three times as often as your company's name.

Making It Pitch-Perfect

Experts offer these other tips for putting together an executive summary that gets attention and gets business:

Use formatting and graphics to highlight your message.

Bullets and headings will make the executive summary easier to skim, and a well-chosen graphic can drive a key point home. If you can find the information in the public record, use a graphic illustrating the client's dilemma.

"This can really rivet their understanding of how bad a situation is," says Sant.

Keep it clear, clean, and to the point.

Strike out jargon, advises Catklaw's Kelly. Her pet peeves include *world-class, turnkey, value-added,* and *leverage* (as a verb). And proofread carefully, says Porter-Roth. "Always have a fresh pair of eyes review the executive summary for grammar, selling themes, and especially overall consistency. Too often the executive summary is a cut-and-paste job and it shows."

While you're in editing mode, make sure your executive summary stays true to its name. "Keep your executive summary short—one to two pages for the first 25 pages of proposal text and an additional page for each 50 pages thereafter," Sant says.

Take advantage of technology.

If you deliver electronically, Kelly says, use the linking functions in Microsoft Word. "Make it easy for them to click to more information later in the document."

Reprint C0308E

Five Quick Ways to Trim Your Writing

• • •

John Clayton

Word comes back from the boss on the report you labored weeks over: "This is good, but it needs to be a lot shorter." You throw up your hands in frustration. She didn't tell you what to cut or how. Not only does your report gather together all the information the committee needs to make a decision on the project, but it gathers that information together well. Every section furthers the argument, you say to yourself; there's nothing extraneous in it.

Similar situations crop up in many business settings. A presentation handout you want to keep on one page. A project description limited to 200 words. An executive summary of a complex, detailed report. Here are some tips for cutting length without losing meaning.

Take a Good, Hard Look at the Structure

Which parts support the roof, and which can be cut away without collapsing the whole structure?

The old advice about previewing and then reviewing your message may be fine for lengthy reports and essays, but when you're squeezed for space, they amount to building three walls to do the job of one. Don't announce what you will say, just say it.

For example, you may have followed your old English teacher's advice to include in your introductory paragraph one sentence previewing each point you will make. Here's an easy cut: Delete the introductory paragraph and jump right into the message.

Additionally, the foundation you built may be more solid than you need. For example, maybe you've included detailed background information. Does your audience really need it all to understand and be persuaded by your argument? If not, summarize it briefly and get right to the bottom line.

Finally, some of your structure may be unnecessary. If a section exists mostly for show, it can go. Cut anything that illuminates something other than your main point.

Stick to Specifics

Specifics make up the meat of your argument, and generalities the carbs; put your writing on a high-protein, low-carb diet. A telling anecdote or statistic will stay with your audience longer than a generality and will usually convey the more general message.

Think of how politicians often expend their precious time in a speech or debate highlighting a specific hero's story. They know that telling a story (of a wounded soldier, laid-off worker, entrepreneur) is the best way to put forward a platform (better weapons, more unemployment insurance, lower taxes).

Use Formatting Creatively

You might first think that adding illustrations or headings to a report will eat up space, but in fact this tactic can help you shave down how many words are needed to get your message across.

Headings

Headings are useful because they clarify a report's organization, eliminate the need for topic sentences, create white space, and help readers skim. But the way they're usually formatted—on a line by themselves, sometimes with a blank line following—takes up a lot of space. If you want the space back without losing the headings, convert them to in-paragraph headings.

Tables

If you want to compare and contrast various options, do so in a table rather than in running text. Just to start with, you won't have to keep repeating the names of the different companies, for instance, or the criteria on which you're judging them. More significantly, a table presents complex comparisons in a succinct way. Your readers can compare and contrast Options A and B, Options B and D, or Options A, B, and C, as they want; you don't have to write out all the similarities and differences between various options.

An added bonus: The audience's expectations change when they look at tables. They don't expect complete sentences, and they may be willing to look at text in a smaller font.

Maps and diagrams

Think how long it takes to write out directions: *Maple St. is the third stoplight. There's a Denny's on one corner and a used-car lot on the other corner, but if you get to the Clarksdale city limits you've gone too far.* A map conveys the same information concisely and accessibly. Flowcharts and organizational charts likewise convey complex relationships in easy-to-understand form.

Emphasis

To make sure your audience remembers what you have to say, you may be tempted to use phrases like *This is the key to the whole thing* or *If you take one message away from this document, let it be the following*. Instead, put that message in boldface and you've conveyed those phrases implicitly.

Downshift Your Tone

There is something about writing a report that causes many people to adopt a formal, bureaucratic tone. When you write this way, you use bigger words, more parenthetical phrases, and a greater number of complex sentences. If you shift to a more informal tone, you may find yourself writing shorter.

Here's one place to start: Use contractions. It's not that changing *cannot* to *can't* and *will not* to *won't* saves so much space, but using contractions will help you avoid the long, formal style of bureaucrats, explains Edward P. Bailey in *Plain English at Work*.

Another way to shift your tone is to speak directly to your audience, using personal pronouns such as *you*. Maybe you had a teacher who didn't allow you to use *you,* so you developed wordy ways to avoid it. For example, *The lights must be turned off before the office is vacated.*

But *you* is fine in most business contexts, and using it can let you write a lot shorter. *You must turn off the lights before you leave.* We've gone from 60 to 45 characters—a savings of 25%.

Cut and Combine

Look over your document sentence by sentence, looking for ways to cut words by combining two sentences into one. Consider these sentences:

> This presentation examines the benefits of outsourcing. It is my recommendation that we reduce overhead by outsourcing noncore processes such as customer service, fulfillment, and other support functions.

The first sentence is dead weight. Cut it out and write instead:

> We could significantly reduce overhead by outsourcing such noncore support functions as customer service and fulfillment.

You've now both announced your topic and stated your position on it with wording that's almost 50% leaner than the original.

When the length of a document doesn't matter to the reader, you insert lots of phrases that help pinpoint what you're talking about. The previous sentence contains examples of such phrases: *of a document* and *to the reader.* You don't always need to be so specific. For instance, if we delete those phrases so that the sentence begins, *When length doesn't matter,* the word count has been significantly reduced without any loss of meaning.

Here are some other ways to crop words:

Drop lengthy titles.

Rather than *Bob Smith, Assistant Vice President for Corporate Communications and Government Relations, says* . . . you could write *spokesperson Bob Smith says.* . . .

Look out for the obvious.

Rather than write, *Obviously, this means we will need to raise prices, which could reduce sales,* write instead, *Our need to raise prices could reduce sales.* Do a search for the word *obvious,* and see if the sentences in which it or *obviously* appears could be trimmed down. After all, if something is obvious, why waste precious space saying it?

Replace long words or phrases with shorter ones. In *Legal Writing in Plain English,* Bryan A. Garner notes some easy ways to tighten up your language. On its own, each such change may save just a little space, but it's like saving pennies: Eventually they add up to something meaningful.

Convert "of" phrases to possessives.

For example, change *the success of the company* to *the company's success.*

Replace bloated phrases with simpler words.

An adequate number of can be replaced with *enough, notwithstanding the fact that* is a windy way of saying *although,* and *during such time as* simply means *while.*

Use active verbs.

Passive constructions require more verbiage. For example, look again at the final example under "Downshift Your Tone." Avoiding *you* required using a passive construction (*The lights must be turned off before the office is vacated*) that was much wordier than the sentence with an active verb (*You must turn off the lights before you leave*).

Never express a number in both digits and words.

There's no need to write *Twelve (12) people attended the meeting;* either the word or the numeral works fine on its own. Your corporate style manual may have specific guidelines on when to express numbers as numerals and when to express them as words, but following two general principles can save you space: (1) Never double up; (2) Always use numerals for large numbers (*200,000,* not *two hundred thousand*).

Some of these tips may sound suspiciously like the general advice you get on how to write well. That's no coincidence: Good writing is concise.

But the problem we set out to solve was that your boss told you to cut your report by 30%. Following these tips can do that for you. And if she comes back to you to say, "You know, that shorter version is a lot better written, too," that will just be a bonus.

For Further Reading

Plain English at Work: A Guide to Business Writing and Speaking by Edward P. Bailey (1996, Oxford University Press)

Legal Writing in Plain English: A Text with Exercises by Bryan A. Garner (2001, University of Chicago Press)

Reprint C0304D

Avoiding Grammatical Goofs and Gaffes

· · ·

Grammar rules can confuse and stymie even accomplished business writers. You want to follow the rules and therefore demonstrate your intelligence and attention to detail. Yet you know you're not familiar with all the rules. Moreover, you see others around you breaking well-known rules all the time (for instance, by splitting infinitives or using sentence fragments). What to do? The articles in this section can help.

Several of the following selections advocate working around grammar problems you're not sure how to solve. For example, by using the word *praise* if you're unsure of whether *complement* or *compliment* is the right synonym, you can avoid an embarrassing mistake. Another article makes the persuasive argument that sometimes it's better *not* to follow a grammar rule slavishly. After all, some rules (such as "Never split an infinitive") are archaic—and following them can give your prose a stilted quality.

Misused Words and Other Writing Gaffes

A Manager's Primer

• • •

Kristen B. Donahue

Managers are valued for their leadership, management skills, and vision, not for their adherence to the rules of grammar and punctuation. And yet the ability to communicate via the written word is crucial. Grammatical mistakes, clunky phrasing, and carelessness can muddle your message and undermine your credibility. And even when there's nothing at stake, writing errors can just be plain embarrassing. A real-life case in point: an e-mail informing employees of computer network problems that was supposed to read, "We apologize for any inconvenience this may cause," actually read, "We apologize for any incontinence this may cause."

Herewith, then, a simple primer on some common writing mistakes.

Mistaking Wordiness for Erudition

Many people try to impress and establish authority by expressing complex thoughts in long, complex sentences with multisyllabic words. The result is often incomprehensible: *"We have experienced lapses in the optimal performance of the manufacturing equipment in Area Three. It is therefore imperative that we undertake a shutdown of that area effective immediately and initiate an investigation of the situation."* What these hapless writers fail to understand is that the best business writing is invisible, meaning that the message takes center stage, not fancy words: *Manufacturing operations in Area Three will be shut down until we can investigate the source of the performance problems.*

Stating the Obvious

Writers who fall victim to overwriting also tend to pad their sentences with unnecessary words in an attempt to emphasize their point: *Going forward, the company plans to submit four new drugs for approval in 2001. Clearly, the current submission process is inefficient.* In the first sentence, the phrase "going forward" is redundant, and in the second, the thought should be clear enough that "clearly" is unnecessary.

Turning Nouns into Verbs

"Verbifying" nouns is such a common practice these days that the words appear in many dictionaries, so it's a surprise for some people to learn that it's not correct grammar. Grammar purists, however, still frown on this practice, and there's a strong chance your writing audience will react badly to it. Some well-worn noun-verbs to avoid: *impact, incent, architect.*

Subject/Verb Disagreement

Collective nouns like management, team, group, organization, and audience take the singular: *The implementation team meets to discuss strategy once a week. After the meeting it distributes a list of next steps.* They and *their* are never correct with collective nouns. If it sounds funny, rewrite the sentence: *The team members meet. . . . After the meeting they distribute. . . .*

Dodging the Gender Bullet

Many writers, hoping to avoid the gender problem alto-gether, opt for the third person plural: *The customer may not be aware they can request this service.* Alas, this is incor-rect. There are three solutions: use the phrase *he or she,* alternate gender in each example, or rewrite the sentence to make the subject plural: *Customers may not be aware they can request.* . . .

Failing to Proofread

This is the final frontier of good business writing. Intense deadlines, momentary distractions, attempts to multitask—these situations occur often and make it easy to slip up. Spell-checkers can help with simple typos such as misspellings and repeated words, but they are little defense against the equally common "thinkos," such as the inconvenience/incontinence example above. Your only defense against thinkos is a careful read. Set the completed, spell-checked document aside for at least a few minutes, then read through once more with as fresh an eye as possible. This step is especially important when the topic is emotionally charged or very sensitive.

Reprint C0111D

How to Write Correctly Without Knowing the Rules

• • •

John Clayton

You're writing a report on a visit to an affiliate office, and you type the sentence *Everyone here, even she, believes her data are flawed.* You pause, puzzled. Should that be *even her?* It doesn't sound right, but you can't put your finger on why. Stopping to ponder it, and perhaps consult a grammar book, you lose your train of thought. You may soon start wondering if *believes* should be *believe* or if *data are* should be *data is.* Every such mental debate chips away at your productivity—and your confidence in your own writing ability.

The English language, with its endless capacity to absorb influences from a variety of cultures and languages, occasionally presents challenges that can slow down even sophisticated writers. It's a dilemma: poor writing sends bad messages to readers, but stopping to wrestle with the complexities of grammar and usage can waste time and money. The more productive solution is to develop strategies to avoid these quagmires.

There's no shame in doing so—we readily use shortcuts to solve other problems. Think of how you add numbers in your head by grouping tens and hundreds. It's not cheating. The important thing is that the result is correct; you need not demonstrate your knowledge of arithmetic.

The same principle holds for composition. You don't have to demonstrate your knowledge of obscure grammar rules. You can simply "round up" to an equivalent phrase that's easier to handle. By rewriting the sentence, you avoid the complicating issue.

Let's return to the question of whether the pronoun in the example should be *she* or *her*. The "correct" answer is *she* because the pronoun addresses the subject (rather than the object) of the sentence. But you need not know this to write a correct sentence. You can simply avoid the issue by using the person's name again instead of the pronoun. *Everyone here, even Linda, believes her data are flawed.*

Now, for those who are hung up on the verb *believes:* it's correct, because *everyone* is an indefinite pronoun and indefinite pronouns nearly always take singular verbs. But again, you can rewrite the sentence to avoid that construction. *Each person here, even Linda, believes her data are flawed.*

Finally, there's the question of what verb to use with *data.* Officially, *data*—like *criteria* and *media*—is a plural noun and thus takes a plural verb: *data are.* But so few people know or use this rule that many (though not all) experts now accept the singular: *data is.*

Given this wishy-washy state of affairs, the best solution may be an avoidance strategy: to rewrite the sentence so that *data* doesn't require a verb. *Each person here, even Linda, believes there are flaws in her data* or . . . *flaws weaken her data.*

If you don't know the grammar rule, recast the sentence so that you can use grammar you do know. Just be careful not to change the meaning of the original statement.

Let's look at some other examples.

The proposal will sink or swim on its merits. Does *its* need an apostrophe? The rule is that *it's* substitutes for *it is,* whereas *its* indicates possession (so the sentence is correct as written). But if you're not sure about the rule, instead of looking it up, simply rewrite the sentence! *The merits of the proposal will determine if it sinks or swims.*

The effect of the regulation will be to raise costs. Is that *effect* or *affect?* If it's a noun, it's most likely *effect.* (*Affect* is used as a noun only in specialized contexts to refer to the manifestation of emotion.) So the sentence is correct as written. But why not avoid the issue? *The result of the regulation will be to raise costs.*

This example demonstrates how you can use the same avoidance strategy with your choice of words. In *The Art of Spelling,* Marilyn vos Savant notes that homophones (words that sound alike but have different spellings and meanings) cause particular problems because your spell-checker won't see anything wrong when you misuse them. Commonly confused homophones, she says, include *capital/capitol, complement/compliment,* and *palate/palette.*

When you come across a problem word, focus on your intended meaning instead of the word itself—then you will be better able to think of a good substitute. Instead of *capitol,* use *State House* or *Congress;* instead of *capital,* use *Washington* or *Albany.* Instead of *compliment,* use *praise;* instead of *palette,* use *available colors.*

Remember that the point of writing is not to show off how many words or rules you know. Your obligation to your readers is simply to master the subject under consideration and communicate your knowledge of it clearly.

Too often it seems that usage problems arise from precisely the desire to overreach, to show off knowledge. Take the abbreviations *i.e.* and *e.g.,* which are commonly confused and often incorrectly punctuated. You can avoid them by using the phrases *in other words* (for *i.e.*) and *for example* (for *e.g.*). After all, that's what those terms mean! Why bother to dress up those meanings with Latin abbreviations that your audience only vaguely understands?

Or how about good old *who* and *whom?* In *The Manager's Guide to Business Writing*, Suzanne D. Sparks notes that *who* and *whom* are a source of endless problems. She cites the example: *There's a bonus for whoever finishes on time*. Should that be *whomever?* Who cares? (Or, if you prefer, To whom does it matter?) Let's just rewrite the sentence! *If you finish on time, you get a bonus*.

All you need to know is how to identify the problem. You don't need to know how to fix the problem, just how to steer clear of it. For example, the *who*-versus-*whom* problem arises when your question contains prepositions, such as *to, for,* or *against*. So when you see that you've written a question with prepositions, rewrite it without them. For example, rather than *Who are you speaking to?* (which is, to grammatical perfectionists, incorrect) or *To whom are you speaking?* (the correct, though almost too formal, version), write *Who is your audience?*

Note that the focus here is on *re*-writing the sentences. It's OK to write them incorrectly the first time. In fact, it's better to write them incorrectly so you can focus on your train of thought first. That's why you go back and proofread later. It's easier to rewrite several sentences in a second draft than to keep interrupting your thought process to write them perfectly the first time.

Many writers will do anything to avoid mastering the most intricate grammar rules—rules that are in constant flux anyway as usage changes. If you're one of those writers, you may find that devising avoidance strategies will save you time and frustration.

For Further Reading

The Manager's Guide to Business Writing by Suzanne D. Sparks (1998, McGraw-Hill)

The Art of Spelling: The Madness and the Method by Marilyn vos Savant (2001, W.W. Norton)

Reprint C0209E

Is Following the Rules Tripping Up Your Message?

• • •

Christina Bielaszka-DuVernay

Will the sky fall if you end a sentence with a preposition? Will gravity fail if you split an infinitive? No, of course not.

In fact, your most sophisticated readers won't even bat an eye. And it's not because they've become so accustomed to the shortcuts and improvisations of e-mail that they don't notice when someone breaks a rule. They still notice, all right. It's just that they know that some "rules" aren't rules at all—and never were.

These nonrules are known as "superstitions" among the grammar and usage set, and they may be preventing your writing from being as strong, direct, and effective as it can be. Here are the four most common:

Never end a sentence with a preposition.

This is one of the most enduring of superstitions, despite centuries of commentary trying to dispel it.

The origins of this bugaboo lie in etymology and the origins of English grammar, explains Bryan A. Garner, widely respected language authority and author of the excellent *A Dictionary of Modern American Usage*.

In Latin, *preposition* means "stand before," and in Latin a preposition does indeed stand before other words; it's the one part of speech that can't end a Latin sentence.

But English is not Latin. Although English grammar is modeled on Latin grammar, the languages are very different and some rules just don't translate well.

Criticized for ending a sentence with a preposition, Winston Churchill is said to have quipped, "That is the type of arrant pedantry up with which I shall not put." As this absurdly stilted sentence demonstrates, the syntactical contortions necessary to keep a sentence ending preposition-free result in awkward, turgid prose—not the best vehicle for your message.

Never split an infinitive.

The fact is, some infinitives beg to be split. Consider this sentence: *Our CEO expects to more than double revenues this year.*

Try rewriting it so as to eliminate the split infinitive; there's no way to do it without losing the precise meaning of the original.

Here is another example: *We are trying to immediately solve any customer-service problems that arise.*

Transposing *to* and *immediately* confuses the meaning—*immediately* seems to modify *are trying*. Placing *immediately* after *solve* makes the sentence stilted. And moving *immediately* to the end of the sentence is no good, because there it appears to modify *arise*.

With split infinitives, the best bet is to steer a middle course. If you can avoid a split infinitive without altering meaning, introducing ambiguity, or interrupting flow, you should do so, advises Garner.

Never begin a sentence with *and* or *but*.

Go ahead and do it—you'll be in good company. The *Oxford English Dictionary* cites sentences beginning with *and* that date back to the 10th century.

A scholar in the 1960s, says Garner, studied the work

of top-flight writers—H.L. Mencken and Lionel Trilling among them—and found that nearly 9% of their sentences began with *and* or *but*. Garner's own research has turned up similar results.

Some writers substitute *however* for *but* at the beginning of a sentence, believing that by so doing they're hewing to the grammatical line. What they're doing is stalling the progress of their prose. *But* at the beginning of a sentence keeps things zipping nicely along, while *however*—followed by its obligatory comma—is a verbal speed bump, jarring the reader and slowing him down.

Never write a one-sentence paragraph.

Varied paragraph length, like varied sentence length, is a hallmark of a skilled stylist. Writing a one-sentence paragraph is an excellent way to grab the reader's attention or emphasize an important point.

Just don't overdo it.

For Further Reading

A Dictionary of Modern American Usage by Bryan A. Garner (1998, Oxford University Press)

Reprint C0212F

About the Contributors

John Clayton is a writer based in Montana. His clients range from A.T. Kearney to National Geographic.

Nick Wreden is a consultant based in Atlanta.

Beverly Ballaro has taught language, literature, and writing courses at Yale, Cornell, and Wheelock College.

Christina Bielaszka-DuVernay is a contributor to *Harvard Management Update*.

Janice Obuchowski is a contributor to *Harvard Management Update*.

Nick Morgan is a contributor to *Harvard Management Update*.

Holly Weeks is a Cambridge-based communications consultant.

Richard Bierck is a business writer based in Princeton, NJ. His work has appeared in *U.S. News & World Report, Bloomberg Personal Finance,* and *Parade*.

Stever Robbins is president of VentureCoach, Inc., an executive coaching firm.

Susan G. Parker is a freelance reporter living and working in Cambridge, MA.

Theodore Kinni has written or ghostwritten seven books.

Kristen B. Donahue is a contributor to *Harvard Management Update*.

Harvard Business Review Paperback Series

The Harvard Business Review Paperback Series offers the best thinking on cutting-edge management ideas from the world's leading thinkers, researchers, and managers. Designed for leaders who believe in the power of ideas to change business, these books will be useful to managers at all levels of experience, but especially senior executives and general managers. In addition, this series is widely used in training and executive development programs.

These books are priced at US$19.95
Price subject to change.

Title	Product #
Harvard Business Review **Interviews with CEOs**	3294
Harvard Business Review on **Advances in Strategy**	8032
Harvard Business Review on **Appraising Employee Performance**	7685
Harvard Business Review on **Becoming a High Performance Manager**	1296
Harvard Business Review on **Brand Management**	1445
Harvard Business Review on **Breakthrough Leadership**	8059
Harvard Business Review on **Breakthrough Thinking**	181X
Harvard Business Review on **Building Personal and Organizational Resilience**	2721
Harvard Business Review on **Business and the Environment**	2336
Harvard Business Review on **The Business Value of IT**	9121
Harvard Business Review on **Change**	8842
Harvard Business Review on **Compensation**	701X
Harvard Business Review on **Corporate Ethics**	273X
Harvard Business Review on **Corporate Governance**	2379
Harvard Business Review on **Corporate Responsibility**	2748
Harvard Business Review on **Corporate Strategy**	1429
Harvard Business Review on **Crisis Management**	2352
Harvard Business Review on **Culture and Change**	8369
Harvard Business Review on **Customer Relationship Management**	6994
Harvard Business Review on **Decision Making**	5572

To order, call 1-800-668-6780, or go online at www.HBSPress.org

Title	Product #
Harvard Business Review on **Developing Leaders**	5003
Harvard Business Review on **Doing Business in China**	6387
Harvard Business Review on **Effective Communication**	1437
Harvard Business Review on **Entrepreneurship**	9105
Harvard Business Review on **Finding and Keeping the Best People**	5564
Harvard Business Review on **Innovation**	6145
Harvard Business Review on **The Innovative Enterprise**	130X
Harvard Business Review on **Knowledge Management**	8818
Harvard Business Review on **Leadership**	8834
Harvard Business Review on **Leadership at the Top**	2756
Harvard Business Review on **Leadership in a Changed World**	5011
Harvard Business Review on **Leading in Turbulent Times**	1806
Harvard Business Review on **Managing Diversity**	7001
Harvard Business Review on **Managing High-Tech Industries**	1828
Harvard Business Review on **Managing People**	9075
Harvard Business Review on **Managing Projects**	6395
Harvard Business Review on **Managing the Value Chain**	2344
Harvard Business Review on **Managing Uncertainty**	9083
Harvard Business Review on **Managing Your Career**	1318
Harvard Business Review on **Marketing**	8040
Harvard Business Review on **Measuring Corporate Performance**	8826
Harvard Business Review on **Mergers and Acquisitions**	5556
Harvard Business Review on **Mind of the Leader**	6409
Harvard Business Review on **Motivating People**	1326
Harvard Business Review on **Negotiation**	2360
Harvard Business Review on **Nonprofits**	9091
Harvard Business Review on **Organizational Learning**	6153
Harvard Business Review on **Strategic Alliances**	1334
Harvard Business Review on **Strategies for Growth**	8850
Harvard Business Review on **Teams That Succeed**	502X
Harvard Business Review on **Turnarounds**	6366
Harvard Business Review on **What Makes a Leader**	6374
Harvard Business Review on **Work and Life Balance**	3286

Harvard Business Essentials

In the fast-paced world of business today, everyone needs a personal resource—a place to go for advice, coaching, background information, or answers. The Harvard Business Essentials series fits the bill. Concise and straightforward, these books provide highly practical advice for readers at all levels of experience. Whether you are a new manager interested in expanding your skills or an experienced executive looking to stay on top, these solution-oriented books give you the reliable tips and tools you need to improve your performance and get the job done. Harvard Business Essentials titles will quickly become your constant companions and trusted guides.

These books are priced at US$19.95, except as noted.
Price subject to change.

Title	Product #
Harvard Business Essentials: **Negotiation**	1113
Harvard Business Essentials: **Managing Creativity and Innovation**	1121
Harvard Business Essentials: **Managing Change and Transition**	8741
Harvard Business Essentials: **Hiring and Keeping the Best People**	875X
Harvard Business Essentials: **Finance for Managers**	8768
Harvard Business Essentials: **Business Communication**	113X
Harvard Business Essentials: **Manager's Toolkit ($24.95)**	2896
Harvard Business Essentials: **Managing Projects Large and Small**	3213
Harvard Business Essentials: **Creating Teams with an Edge**	290X
Harvard Business Essentials: **Entrepreneur's Toolkit**	4368
Harvard Business Essentials: **Coaching and Mentoring**	435X
Harvard Business Essentials: **Crisis Management**	4376
Harvard Business Essentials: **Time Management**	6336
Harvard Business Essentials: **Power, Influence, and Persuasion**	631X
Harvard Business Essentials: **Strategy**	6328
Harvard Business Essentials: **Decision Making**	7618
Harvard Business Essentials: **Marketer's Toolkit**	7626
Harvard Business Essentials: **Performance Management**	9428

The Results-Driven Manager

The Results-Driven Manager series collects timely articles from *Harvard Management Update* and *Harvard Management Communication Letter* to help senior to middle managers sharpen their skills, increase their effectiveness, and gain a competitive edge. Presented in a concise, accessible format to save managers valuable time, these books offer authoritative insights and techniques for improving job performance and achieving immediate results.

These books are priced at US$14.95
Price subject to change.

Management Dilemmas:
Case Studies from the Pages of
Harvard Business Review

When facing a difficult management challenge, wouldn't it be great if you could turn to a panel of experts to help guide you to the right decision? Now you can, with books from the Management Dilemmas series. Drawn from the pages of Harvard Business Review, each insightful guide poses a range of familiar and perplexing business situations and shares the wisdom of a small group of leading experts on how each of them would resolve the problem. Engagingly written, these interactive, solutions-oriented collections allow readers to match wits with the experts. They are designed to help managers hone their instincts and problem-solving skills to make sound judgment calls on everyday management dilemmas.

These books are priced at US$19.95
Price subject to change.

Title	Product #
Management Dilemmas: **When Change Comes Undone**	5038
Management Dilemmas: **When Good People Behave Badly**	5046
Management Dilemmas: **When Marketing Becomes a Minefield**	290X
Management Dilemmas: **When People Are the Problem**	7138
Management Dilemmas: **When Your Strategy Stalls**	712X

How to Order

Harvard Business School Press publications are available worldwide from your local bookseller or online retailer.
You can also call

1-800-668-6780

Our product consultants are available to help you
8:00 a.m.–6:00 p.m., Monday–Friday, Eastern Time.
Outside the U.S. and Canada, call: 617-783-7450
Please call about special discounts for quantities greater than ten.

You can order online at

www.HBSPress.org